The Ultimate
OPTIONS
TRADING
Strategy Guide
For Beginners

Learn about Options Trading and learn six
great strategies to help you profit from it

ROJI ABRAHAM

The Ultimate Options Trading Strategy Guide for Beginners

Copyright © 2017 by Roji Abraham

ISBN-13: 978-1548637804

ISBN-10: 1548637807

Contents

Introduction

Congratulations on purchasing this book and welcome to the world of options trading!

Before diving into the main content, here's a personal anecdote to start with.

It was the third week of January 2008.

My cousin and I were sitting glued to our television set catching every word of the screaming presenter on the CNN-IBN financial news channel in disbelief. The panic that had struck us a day earlier had robbed us both of our sleep and our appetite. We groaned as we saw the benchmark index of the stock market nosedive again - the second day in a row.

The fears of a global recession in the wake of the sub-prime crisis had hit the Indian stock market too. On the 22nd of January, trading on the National Stock Exchange (NSE) was suspended after its benchmark index plunged by 10% in the first few minutes of trading –it had hit an extremely rare phenomenon called a lower circuit!

Stock markets globally were taking a beating and the months that followed were the worst days in decades for stock traders and investors globally.

We were, at the time, two bachelors in our mid-twenties - graduate engineers who worked for top-notch software companies in the city. The two of us shared an apartment and we were both stock market junkies. In those days, when we got back after work, we had only one thing to talk about- the stock market. We discussed about it for hours on end and checked our open positions every evening before deciding which wagon to jump into the next day.

We had started share trading only a year earlier and had entered the derivatives segment (also called Futures and Options or F&O) after trading stocks for just a few months. My cousin preferred Futures while I leaned towards Options.

As incredibly naïve newcomers at that time, we had no real trading strategy. We cherry-picked ostensibly good stocks and bought naked (unprotected) Options or Futures and kept our fingers crossed. We had a run of good luck and an excellent bull market in 2007 rewarded us with some enviable profits for a while – at times even surpassing our monthly income from our full-time jobs. The money was easy – too easy in fact.

But when the stock markets eventually crashed, it came like a cold hard slap on our faces. By the time we cut our losses and exited, we had lost hundreds of thousands of Rupees because none of our high-risk positions were hedged (protected). I had practically gambled away more than a couple of years' worth of savings. It was far worse for my cousin though – he lost more than four times the amount I lost (trading Futures was undoubtedly riskier) and had to take a sizeable loan to pay off his debts.

We both stopped trading then and stopped talking about the stock market following that incident. Though we moved on with our lives and live in different countries today, whenever we run into each other occasionally, we refrain from discussing our old painful financial blunder. That crash of 2008 had left an indelible scar on our lives.

Our story wasn't an isolated one and many people suffered far worse. A lot of stock traders, including retail traders and part-timers, lost a fortune in the 2008 crisis and many others went bust. Traders who survived the 2008 stock market crash were left with their own stories to tell – and they are unlikely to be happy ones.

Nevertheless, even in that crisis, there were prudent traders who escaped with little damage and there were a few wise ones who actually profited too!

I stayed off options trading for a rather long time and when I decided to re-enter trading, I was determined not to repeat my past mistakes. For that to happen, I realised I'd have to think and behave like the real 'pros'. Such traders, as I came to know, approached trading quite differently from the average retail trader – while they consistently made profits irrespective of the market situation, they were always prepared for any unforeseen disastrous events.

I researched for the best study material out there and sifted through numerous books and online knowledge base articles – including the good, the bad, and occasionally, the brutally ugly. I also enrolled for paid trainings with some excellent traders who were also educators and made it a habit to regularly listen and learn from their videos and podcasts. I also started creating my own spread sheets for testing strategies to figure out what worked best in the real world. Slowly my perceptions and attitude towards trading itself changed and so did my fortunes.

The irony is that the knowledge I came to possess was always out there and yet I had never tried to seek it out earlier because of the false sense of confidence I got from my winning trades when I started out – most of which were just a result of good luck.

The silver lining in that crash of 2008 was that it forced me to become a far more knowledgeable and better trader.

Today, I know for certain that with most trades I enter, I will earn small steady sums consistently or at least break even. Even if I decide to take a chance with a riskier trade and make a wrong trade choice, my trade will always be hedged to ensure that my losses are always limited to a sum I can afford to lose. I also know today that were another major crash to happen, I would be protected because each trade I make is sufficiently hedged.

Following my successful re-entry into the world of options trading, I started speaking with various other traders and I realised most of them bled money over the long term because they had very elementary knowledge of options trading and were often just oblivious to the existence of practical strategies – in other words many of them were doing what I did in 2008. I also realised that many such traders seldom come across a basic resource that could teach them about options trading without all the technical gobbledygook intelligible only to geeks.

And that was the realisation that led me to the conceptualisation of this book.

This book is a product of all the experience and learning I have gained over many years and it has been written in the simplest way possible to teach beginners about options trading and how to earn from it using a set of strong strategies. Even if you have no clue what options are right now, this book will teach you the necessary basics, as long as you show patience and a willingness to learn.

While nobody can accurately predict stock market behaviour, the knowledge you will gain through this book, when applied diligently, will make you a much better trader, protect your money better, irrespective of the stock market's whims, and will earn you far more consistent profits than the average Joe who throws in his money like he rolls dice, month after month and still ends up poorer with passing time.

I truly believe that this book will change the way in which you perceive options trading altogether and wish you success in all your trades ahead.

Roji Abraham
Jul 2017

What You Will Learn in This Book

You really do not need to be an investment banker or a financial whiz kid to earn consistently from the markets. All you need is some sound knowledge of the basics of options trading, and an understanding of the right set of options trading strategies and when to apply them. Once you have these you will realise that earning money in the stock market isn't that hard as it seems to be and it isn't a gamble after all.

This book begins with a simple explanation of what options really are in layman's terms and then goes on to explain the various types of options and also the various common terms used in options trading that any trader must know at all times.

Moving forward from that point, this book will show you the most common mistakes made by the over-zealous new traders and how to avoid them.

Finally, the book will then illustrate, with examples, six of the most popular and effective strategies used by options traders to create wealth, with case-studies to help enhance your knowledge further on each of those options trading strategies.

Chapter 1: Understanding Stock Options

What are Stock Options?

You probably know what a stock/share of a company is - in the simplest of terms, a single share represents a solitary unit of ownership of a company.

Companies offer their shares for sale to raise capital for themselves and such shares (also sometimes referred to as equities) are listed and traded in a stock exchange.

In a stock exchange, many high profile shares that trade in huge volumes may also have derivatives associated with them. A derivative is a contract between two or more parties in which the contract 'derives' its value from an underlying security such as a stock or an index.

The most commonly traded derivatives in the stock market are Futures and Options. They are also commonly referred to as F&O.

Futures contracts are relatively easier to understand when compared to options, but they carry more risk and are less flexible. Nevertheless, discussing futures is beyond the scope of discussion in this book and our focus will be strictly on options.

An option is defined as a type of contract, sold by one party to another that gives the buyer of the option, the right, but not the obligation, to buy or to sell the underlying stock at a pre-determined price.

Options contracts cannot exist indefinitely and every option has an expiry date. The option buyer of a specific option may have a right to exercise his/her option only at the time of expiry of the option, or he/she may have a right to exercise the option at any point in time till the date of expiry (depending on whether the option follows European or American convention – elaborated a little later in this book).

Note: Derivatives can also be based on various other underlying securities such as commodities. However, throughout this book, all examples and scenarios are limited to options trading based on underlying stocks and indices only.

Types of Options

There are fundamentally two different types of options. They are:

1. Call Options – These options give the buyer the right to buy the underlying security at a fixed price.

2. Put Options – These options give the buyer the right to sell the underlying security at a fixed price.

The most important thing to know here is that in the case of a call option, the buyer of the option can only start profiting from that option when the value of the underlying stock/index goes up.

On the other hand, in the case of a put option, the buyer of the option can only start profiting when the value of the underlying stock/index goes down.

European Style and American Style Expiries

There are two different conventions that are followed globally when it comes to exercising an option.

1. European Style Expiry - Call options and put options following the European style expiry are generally denoted by **CE** and **PE**. In this style of expiry, options can be exercised only at the specified time of expiry.

2. American Style Expiry - Call options and put options following the American style expiry are generally denoted by **CA** and **PA**. In this style of expiry, options can be exercised at any time till the specified time of expiry.

The options traded in any stock exchange will follow either of these two conventions, depending on the norm in the country. For example, all options traded in India's NSE follow the European style of expiry.

Basic Terms used in Options Trading

Before getting into examples, here are explanations of the most basic terms one needs to know before getting into options trading.

1. The Strike-Price (SP)

Every options contract will have an associated strike-price. This is the fixed reference price against which settlement takes place at the time the option is exercised or when the option expires. For any given stock/index that is traded in the Futures and Options segment, there will be different options contracts corresponding to various strike-prices. These strike-prices are pre-determined by the stock exchange in which that underlying stock is traded.

For example, the stock of Infosys - the Indian IT giant, that is traded on India's NSE, has a market price of

₹1030 (at the time this book was being written) and has an entire range of associated put and call options available with strike-prices such as 960, 980, 1000, 1020, 1040 etc.

In the case of call options, the strike-price effectively functions as the 'buy price' while the market price of the underlying stock functions as the 'sell price' at the time of settlement or exercising of the options.

In the case of put options, the strike-price effectively functions as the 'sell price' while the market price of the underlying stock functions as the 'buy price' at the time of settlement or exercising of the options.

If you find this information a bit confusing, never mind. You will understand it better once you go through the two scenarios explained in Chapter 2 of this book.

2. The Lot Size

The lot size specifies the fixed number of units of the underlying security that one options contract covers. The lot size is usually determined by the regulatory body within the stock exchange and might vary from stock to stock.

For example, the current lot size for the Indian IT company Infosys, which is traded on the Indian NSE, is 500. So any trader, who buys 1 option of Infosys (irrespective of the type, strike-price or the expiry date), holds buy/sell rights on precisely 500 shares of Infosys. If you buy 1 Infosys call option with a strike-price of 1020, it means your contract gives you the right to buy 500 shares of Infosys at strike-price of 1020. Alternately, if you buy 1 Infosys put option with the strike-price of 1000, your contract gives you the right to sell 500 shares of Infosys at 1000. Since the lot size is fixed at 500, you cannot have an option to control only, say for example,

200 shares or 150 shares through an option – you will always be buying/selling in multiples of 500 only.

The market lot sizes for stocks traded in F&O are revised by the stock exchange from time to time.

Note: In the US NYSE, the lot size is standardised at 100 – in other words, a single options contract entitles the options buyer to 100 shares of the underlying stock/index.

3. The Premium

The premium is simply the amount of money an option buyer pays <u>per share</u> when buying an option (or the amount of money an option seller receives per share for selling an option).

The premium of an option at any point in time is dependent on using various parameters (often referred to as the Options Greeks – something we will cover later on).

The total cost of any options contract, therefore, will be the premium multiplied by the lot size for that underlying. For example: If the premium of an Infosys call option with strike-price 1040 is ₹5, then the cost of that options contract is ₹5 x 500 (lot size) = ₹2,500.

4. The Expiry Date

Every single option has an expiry date.

Expiry of options traded in any exchange could happen on a weekly, monthly, or even quarterly basis. Nevertheless, these dates of expiry follow a rigid calendar determined by the exchange in which the options are traded.

For example: the options for the Bank Nifty (an index of Bank stocks), traded on the Indian NSE, has a weekly expiry and any Bank Nifty option slated for expiry in a given week will always expire on the Thursday of that week (if Thursday is a holiday, expiry takes place the previous day). Similarly, all monthly options traded on the Indian NSE, slated for expiry in a given month, expire on the last Thursday of that month.

At any point in time, there could be multiple monthly contracts available for a given stock depending on the exchange in which that stock is traded.

For example: Stock options for any stock trading on the NSE are available for 3 consecutive trading months at any point in time. So if you are currently in the month of March 2017 (any day before the last Thursday), you would be able to trade monthly options for the months of March 2017, April 2017 and May 2017 and all these options expire on the last Thursday of their corresponding month. When the options for March 2017 expire, the options for June will be made available for trading in the NSE, and so on and so forth.

Chapter 2: Simplified Examples of Options Trades

It is sometimes difficult for a beginner to understand options trading and the various associated terms without viewing them in the context of an actual trade.

Therefore, in this section you will get to read about two different trades involving a cattle breeder and cattle traders - trades that will help you understand the connection between options trading and physical trading in the real world.

The first trade is an analogy of a typical call option trade while the second example is an analogy of a put option trade.

Once you read through these examples, you will be able to easily understand how call options and put options work. These examples should also make it easy for you to comprehend the various terms used in trading.

Trade 1 : Bob's Call Option Trade

Jacob is a farmer and a cattle breeder who owns several dairy cows. Bob, who is an acquaintance of Jacob, is a trader of farm animals.

One day Bob gets a tip from a friend that the town's main dairy was negotiating a deal with a large international chocolate manufacturing company. If the deal were to materialise, the chocolate company would triple the quantity of milk they purchase from the dairy every day. To meet this increase in demand, the dairy would also have to increase milk production, and for increasing production they would have to purchase a large number of dairy cows at short notice – a move that could result in a substantial increase in cow prices locally.

Bob realised he could make some excellent profits if he bought some cows from Jacob and then sold them after the prices went up. However, Bob wasn't completely certain about this tip and did not want to buy cows upfront at the full price of $2,000 (which was the market price for a dairy cow at that time) and later sell out for a loss if the price did not rise as expected.

Therefore, Bob approaches Jacob and makes him a unique offer.

Bob tells Jacob that he will pay the latter a sum of $50 upfront for the right to buy one of his cows at the prevailing market price of $2,000, for the next 30 days. Also, Jacob would be under no obligation to return that amount if Bob no longer wanted to exercise his right (in the event that cow prices dropped below $2,000).

Jacob saw no reason for cow prices rising anytime soon and was therefore glad to sign a contract to receive $50 from trader Bob in exchange for giving Bob the right to buy a cow at $2,000 for the next 30 days.

However, Jacob puts forth a condition that the proposed contract should cover 5 cows and not just 1 cow and that meant Bob, would have to pay a total of $250 for the right to purchase 5 cows for a 30-day period.

Bob agrees to Jacob's condition and therefore, Jacob pockets Bob's $250 and then signs the contract - the contract that gave Bob the right (but not the obligation) to buy 5 of Jacob's cows at the price of $2,000 for the next 30 days.

Bob knew that in the next 30 days the market price of cows would either rise (as per his expectations), or continue to stay the same, or perhaps even fall (in the worst case scenario).

If the market price for cows stayed the same at $2,000, or fell below that value in the next 30 days, Bob would have to simply forfeit the $250 he paid Jacob to get the agreement in place. Bob was under no obligation to buy cows at a lower price and hence his losses will be curtailed to $250 only – the money he paid Jacob to sign the contract.

On the other hand, if the market price for cows did go up within the next 30 days, Bob would approach Jacob to get 5 cows at $2,000 each and Jacob would be contractually obliged to sell the cows at $2,000, irrespective of how much more the cows were worth at that time.

Bob waits.

Three weeks after the contract was put in place, the town dairy signed a deal with the chocolate company to increase their daily supply of milk to the chocolate company by almost 4 times. To meet that demand the dairy started purchasing a large number of dairy cows at increasingly higher rates that resulted in the prices of dairy cows surging by almost 25% in the locality.

Following this price surge, Bob goes to Jacob and exercises his right to buy the 5 cows at $2,000 each. Bob then goes ahead and sells these cows to the dairy at $2,500 each.

Bob, thereby, makes a total profit of $2,250 for these 5 cows ($500 times 5 less the $250 for the contract amount he paid Jacob).

The trade that took place between Bob and Jacob is representative of how an options trade works and if we apply stock market terms into the afore-mentioned scenario then:

- A single cow represents one particular underlying **Share/Stock**.

- Bob is the **Buyer** of the contract and Jacob is the **Seller**. Since this contract gives the buyer the right to buy – this contract is a **Call Option**.

- $2,000 represents the **Market Price** of the share of the given company (at the time the agreement was put in place).

- $2,000 also represents the **Strike-Price** (SP) or the pre-determined price at which the proposed trade would take place between the **buyer** (Bob) and the **seller** (Jacob) – remember that Jacob paid $50 to purchase a cow at a <u>fixed price of $2,000</u>.

- The $50 paid against each cow is called the **Premium.**

- The number **5** indicates the **Lot Size** of the contract – it is the fixed number of shares that an individual options contract covers.

- Lastly, the 30 days in this scenario denotes the **Time to Expiry** of the options contract.

Hope you have perfectly understood how a call option works now.

If you are a little unclear on this still, try reading this entire section one more time and try correlating the various terms with what they actually represented in the Bob-Jacob trade and you should understand the concept of a call option trade without any further difficulty.

Note: In this example, Bob had the right to exercise his option at the time during the 30 day period – this is representative of American style options. Had this trade followed the European style, Bob would have had to wait till the end of the 30 days to exercise his option.

Let's continue with this storyline in the next section to illustrate a put option. Now that you understood how a call option works, the logic behind the working of a put option should come to you much easier.

Trade 2: Jacob's Put Option Trade

After being forced to sell 5 of his cows at a price lesser than the market price due to his contractual obligation, a rather disappointed Jacob starts thinking.

From his experience, Jacob has seen that in situations where livestock prices increase sharply due to some change in the environment, the prices eventually come down marginally before reaching stability.

However, Jacob wasn't certain if cow prices had hit the ceiling yet – if he sold off his cows right away and prices continued to rise he would miss a chance for selling at even better prices. The market price for a cow was currently at $2,500 and Jacob wanted to wait for a couple of weeks and see if it went up any further. If the prices were already at a high and if they dropped sharply, Jacob wanted to ensure that he could sell a few cows for at least $2,400.

Considering his predicament, Jacob decides to get into a contract similar to the one he had earlier signed with Bob. However, this time, he would be the 'buyer' of the right – the right to sell cows at a fixed price (unlike the right to buy that Bob purchased from him).

For this purpose, Jacob approaches Chad, a livestock trader in the local market, and offers him a deal. The deal was that, for the next 60 days, Jacob would have a right to sell Chad 10 cows at $2,400 each. And to own that right,

Jacob would pay $30 per cow - a sum total of $300 for 10 cows.

Chad agrees and signs up for the deal and pockets the $300 since he didn't expect prices to fall from $2,500, let alone fall below $2,400. As long as cow prices stayed above $2,400 for the next 2 months (which Chad thought was very likely), he had nothing to lose.

A month and half later, Jacob's prediction turned out to be right and cow prices dropped down to $2,250.

Therefore, Jacob goes to Chad and exercises his right to sell the cows at $2,400.

Since Chad was contractually obliged to buy the cows at $2,400, he has no choice but to buy the cows at the fixed price despite the cows being worth $150 less in the market. Jacob thereby profits by $1200 ($150 x 10 less the $300 paid for the contract) off his trade.

Like we did last time, let's apply the various stock market terms to this trade too:

- A single cow represents one particular underlying **Share/Stock**.

- Jacob is the **Buyer** of the contract while Chad is the **Seller**. Since this contract gives the buyer the right to sell – this contract is a **Put Option**.

- $2,500 - the price of the cow, represents the **Market Price** of a share (at the time the agreement was put in place).

- $2,400 represents the **Strike-Price** (SP) or the pre-determined price at which the proposed trade would take place between the **Buyer** (Jacob) and the **Seller** (Chad).

- The $30 paid against each cow is the **Premium.**

- The number **10** indicates the **Lot Size** of the contract.

- Lastly, the 60 days in this scenario denotes the **Time to Expiry** of the options contract.

If you aren't still completely clear on the difference between call options and put options and all the various terms we have used so far, do go through these two examples one more time because you need to be completely thorough with your understanding of these trades to understand the strategies that will be taught in Chapter 7.

Chapter 3: Some More Basics

A few more basic concepts you need to understand are explained below:

ITM, OTM and ATM options

ITM (in-the-money), OTM (out-of-the-money), and ATM (at-the-money) are three acronyms that will be frequently referred to in options trading.

ITM options are options that have an intrinsic value. In other words, if they were to be exercised at that point, they would yield some money. Any call option with a strike-price less than the market price of the underlying stock/index is an ITM option. Any put option that has a strike-price greater than the market price of the underlying stock/index is an ITM option. The intrinsic value of any ITM option is the positive difference between its underlying stock's market price and the option's strike-price.

Let's put it this way – when a stock's price rises and crosses the strike-price of an associated call option, then that call option becomes ITM. Similarly, when a stock's price falls below the strike-price of an associated put option, then that put option becomes ITM.

For example, if Stock 'X' is trading at 500, then any put option of X with a strike-price greater than 500 is an ITM option and any call option of X with a strike-price less than 500 is an ITM option.

OTM options are the opposite of ITM options. The do not have any intrinsic value. At the time of expiry, every single OTM option expires worthless. Any call option with its strike-price greater than the market price of its underlying stock/index and any put option with its strike-price less than the market price of its underlying stock/index are OTM options.

For example, if stock 'Y' is trading at 500, then all call options of Y with a strike-price greater than 500 and all put options of Y with a strike-price less than 500 are OTM options.

ATM options are such options for which the strike-prices are currently the same as the underlying's market price. Therefore, an ATM option can easily become an OTM option or an ITM option with any change in the market price of the underlying.

Here's a quick reference chart that depicts these three types of options:

	Call Option	Put Option
ITM	SP of Option<MP of Stock	SP of Option>MP of Stock
OTM	SP of Option>MP of Stock	SP of Option<MP of Stock
ATM	SP of Option = MP of Stock	SP of Option = MP of Stock

Where SP = Strike-Price, MP = Market Price

The main thing you should know is that at the time of expiry only ITM options would have any associated value while at that time OTM and ATM options would be worthless.

When to exit an Options Trade

In our examples from Chapter 2, we saw how options were exercised successfully. In the real world however, few traders would wait till the expiry date to take home their profits.

Squaring off the options contract early when in profit, instead of waiting for a chance to exercise the option, makes a lot of sense – this is especially true for European style options in which the exercising of an option can be done only at time of expiry.

Either way, irrespective of whether a given option follows the American or European style, it is far more prudent to square-off a trade, when in profit, rather than waiting till expiry to exercise the option and risk losing that profit (or even ending in a loss) in the event of a reversal in the direction of the underlying stock.

Note: After you enter an options trade, you exit that trade by squaring-off your position – this means if you are a buyer, you have to sell to close your position, and if you are a seller, you have to buy to close your position. However, at the time of expiry, if you haven't closed an open position, your position gets automatically squared-off based on the price of the underlying stock/index at the time of expiry.

Meanwhile, let's get back to our old friend Bob and his trade to illustrate the point discussed earlier.

We know what happened after Bob bought a call option from Jacob - the market price for a cow eventually rose to $2,500 from the original $2,000 and Bob exercised his option, claimed his cows, and sold them off at the market price, thereby closing his trade for a handsome profit.

If this particular example was an actual stock market trade and if Bob was dealing with a stock market option, then Bob would have had the ability to exercise his option before the expiry date only if his options contract followed the American style of expiry.

In the event that Bob had an options contract that could only be exercised at the time of expiry (European style), and his position was already in profits well before the expiry date, he would not have ideally waited till the expiry date to book his profit. He would have booked profit much earlier by selling off the options contract itself.

If you remember correctly, when Bob bought the option from Jacob, he paid a premium of $50 for the option (the overall contract amount was $250 since it covered 5 cows) and Bob's contract entitled him to buy Jacob's cows at $2,000 each. At that time, the market price for a cow was also $2,000. Therefore, in options terminology, we can say the market price of the stock was equal to the strike-price of the option when Bob bought his option, or in other words, that particular option was an ATM option.

The last statement also implies that Bob's option had no intrinsic value at the time of purchase. If the market price for a cow hadn't appreciated and had remained at $2,000 for the duration of the contract validity, this option's premium value of $50 would have eroded each day and the option would have eventually expired worthless. Nevertheless, the premium of that option was $50 to begin with because it had one full month remaining for expiry, and therefore, time-value.

In an alternate scenario, let us assume that 10 days after Bob's contract with Jacob was in place, Bob saw that cow prices had already touched $2,300. Since he had 20 more days remaining for expiry, Bob decides he doesn't want to wait till the expiry date and he would rather book a profit immediately by selling the call option itself to a third-party.

Bob bought the option for $50 at a strike-price of $2,000 when the market price of the cow was $2,000. But when the market price for a cow went up to $2,300, the value of the call option itself owned by Bob would also have accordingly risen to about $310.

A rise from $50 to $310 is a rather steep climb up, isn't it?

Did you understand why the premium for Bob's option went up from $50 to $310 when the market price of a cow went up from $2,000 to $2,300?

It's not that complicated actually.

The option premium shot up because it is now deep in-the-money (ITM) and it has an intrinsic value of $300 already (the remaining $10 is time-value) whereas at the time the option was purchased, it was an ATM option and had no intrinsic value but only a time-value of $50.

Previously when the market price of the cow was only $2,000, if Bob had exercised his contract, he would not have made any profit - he'd practically have to buy a cow at $2,000 (strike-price) and sell it at $2,000 (market-price) were he to exercise his option immediately. However, when the market price of the cow went up to $2,300, Bob's contract entitled him to purchase Jacob's cows at the old price of $2,000 and therefore that contract's intrinsic value became $300 – in other words, exercising that option at that point in time would yield a profit of $300 (Market price of $2,300 minus the Strike-price of $2,000).

With 20 days left before the expiry of the contract, there would also be some associated time premium (approximated to $10 in this case) and therefore the value of one single call option contract would have jumped to $310 or so from the original $50.

Therefore, Bob just needed to sell that options contract to another trader at the current value of $310 to bag a profit of $260 on each cow which is covered by the contract ($260 = the current premium value of that call option, $310, minus the premium originally paid, $50). Bob's overall profit therefore would then be $260 x 5 (no. of cows covered as part of that contract) = $1300.

Bob will make a neat profit and the new owner of the options contract Bob originally purchased from Jacob will now have to wait till the time of expiry to exercise that option or alternately, he/she too can sell the contract itself to a fourth person, if a suitable opportunity presents itself.

Having the discipline to sell off a contract when it becomes profitable is important, because if you hold on to it for too long, there is a possibility the tide may turn and you may end up losing a portion of your profits or may even end in a loss. Plus if you are a buyer, then the advantage of selling an option as early as possible will ensure you retain maximum time premium which would otherwise keep eroding everyday as the option approaches expiry.

Note 1: All options have an associated time-value and an intrinsic value - while the former is dependent on how far the option is from its expiry date and becomes zero at expiry, the latter is applicable only for ITM options and would be equal to the difference between the strike-price of that option and the market-price of the underlying.

Note 2: While the example above has mentioned that the premium of the option went from $50 to $310 when the price of a cow went up, the premium amount of $310 was an approximated amount for the sake of general understanding. In reality, the actual amount of appreciation in the premium could vary depending on the various factors that affect the options pricing at that time (these factors are discussed in Chapter 5).

Chapter 4: Why should anybody trade in Options?

These are the 4 main reasons why Options Trading is an attractive proposition for those who are keenly interested in the equity markets.

1. Options Limit Risk

The biggest advantage of buying an option is that your risk is limited to the amount of money you pay as premium.

Think of Bob's Call option trade that we had discussed in Chapter 2.

When Bob thought there was a chance of cow prices going up, he paid money upfront and entered a contract with Jacob to sell him 5 cows at $2,000 each; Bob did not actually buy the cows upfront.

Instead, if Bob had bought 5 cows straightaway from Jacob by paying the entire cost of cows at $10,000 (this is synonymous with regular stock trading where one takes delivery of the stocks bought) and if the price of cows had fallen by $500 instead of going up by $500, he would have lost $2,500. By entering into an option contract, Bob stood to lose a maximum amount of only $250, if cow prices were to fall.

So that was a pretty smart move, wasn't it? That's how an options contract can primarily limit risk.

2. Options Provide better Leverage for Money

Options provide excellent leveraging power and a trader can buy an option position that imitates a stock position almost identically but at a huge cost saving.

Let's go back to Bob's trade.

What would have happened if Bob spotted the opportunity for a profitable trade but had only $1,000 to spare in order to buy cows and did not know about options?

He could not have even bought a single cow for that money and would have lost the opportunity to earn a sizeable profit.

But when Bob decided to buy an options contract instead of buying the actual underlying asset, the dynamics of the trade changed.

The entire investment for Bob in his trade was a paltry $250! In other words, the premium he paid was only the fraction of the total cost of 5 cows for which he bought rights to sell. He practically controlled assets worth $10,000 ($2,000 x 5) by means of that contract he bought for $250.

This is one of the most fantastic advantages of options trading – better leverage for money!

3. Options can provide a higher percentage of returns

An options trader has to pay only a fraction of the asset's value to control the actual asset. This gives the trader a chance to earn much more than what could be earned by purchasing that asset upfront and then selling it.

Let's break this down.

In Bob's trading example, the market price of a cow at the beginning of the trade was $2,000.

If a regular cattle trader, with no knowledge about options trading (unlike our astute Bob) had $2,000 in hand, and believed the price of a cow could go up, he would have been able to buy just one cow from Jacob, and would have made just a profit of $500 when the price of cows went up – a profit of 25% given that his investment was $2,000.

On the other hand if Bob had $2,000, he might have probably used $2,000 to buy 8 options contracts at the premium of $50 that gave him purchasing rights for 40 cows instead.

And given the $500 appreciation for the price of each cow that followed, Bob's profit would have been $18,000 ($500 profit per cow x 40 minus $2,000, the total cost price of the contracts) with an investment of just $2,000.

That's a ridiculously high 900% return for the same amount of money!

4. Options help in hedging Futures or Intraday trades

Many traders often buy or short-sell Futures contracts expecting one particular directional movement or the other. Intraday traders also do something similar – they buy/short-sell a large batch of shares in expectation of either an up move or a down move in the course of the day.

If such traders get their directional call wrong, they could end up facing huge losses because in either case, unless a stop-loss (a point at which you cut losses and get out) is initiated, the potential for profit or loss is more or less unlimited.

No trader will complain about unlimited profits when trading Futures or when trading stocks using intraday margins. But if you were to engage in Futures trading or intraday trading without hedging your positions, whenever you encounter losses, it could go to the extent of wiping out your entire capital and perhaps far more – you could actually end with debts greater than what your overall capital in Futures and intraday trades were because you would have been typically trading using margins (3-4 times the leverage on your existing capital) given by your broker.

If you know how to trade options, you can buy call or put options to insure your trade against unlimited loss – the moment your futures/intraday positions turn against your expectations, the options will start covering your loss.

Note: Technically speaking, unlimited losses can take place only in the case of positions that are shorted (short-sold) because there is no upper limit for the price of any share. However, for a long position, the losses incurred will hit a ceiling once the price of the share reaches 0.00 (while on paper, this is a limit to losses, huge drops in any share associated with a Futures trade would be enormous enough to wreak financial havoc for a trader).

Chapter 5: The Options Greeks

It is essential to have a basic idea of the various factors that determine the price of any given option. Knowledge of these would not only help you gain an all-round understanding of options pricing, but would also help in making better decisions when trading options.

There are primarily 5 underlying factors that determine the price of an option, irrespective of whether it is a put or a call. These factors are collectively called the Options Greeks because each of these is named after a Greek letter. They are described in further detail below:

1. DELTA

Delta signifies the rate of change of an option's premium based on the directional movement of the underlying security.

Since every option has an underlying security (in this book these underlying securities are limited to just stocks and indices), a change in that underlying security causes every option associated with that underlying security to increase or decrease. Delta shows the rate of change of the option for one unit of change in the underlying security.

The value of delta ranges from 0 to 1 for call options and from 0 to -1 for put options. Call option delta values are always positive because an increase in the price of the underlying security causes an increase in the price of its call options. Put option delta values are always negative because an increase in the price of the underlying security causes a decrease in the value of its put options.

Here's an example to help you understand how delta works:

Consider the NSE Index, Nifty, to be trading currently at 9150. If the Nifty 9150 call option with current month's expiry has a delta of 0.5 and the Nifty 9100 put option with the current month's expiry has a delta of -0.35, what would be the change in the prices of these two options if Nifty moves up to 9180, all other factors remaining the same?

Since the Nifty index increased by 30 points (from 9150 to 9180), the 9150 call option having a delta of 0.5 will increase by 15 points (0.5 * 30) and the 9100 put option having a delta of -0.35 will decrease by 10.5 points (-0.35 * 30).

Using Delta as a probability indicator

Another thing you need to know is the delta value is also used as an indicator to determine the probability of an option ending in-the-money (ITM) at the time of expiry.

For example: If a call option has a delta of 0.5, this indirectly implies this call option has a 50% probability of ending ITM by the time of expiry.

While the use of delta as a probability proxy need not be precise, it can be used to give a general idea based on random market movement and an unbiased valuation of options. Using delta as a probability proxy is quite useful when deploying a strategy such as the Iron Condor (discussed later) because, by using the delta as an indicator, a trader can choose the right options to trade that could maximise his profit potential while still maintaining a relatively high probability of success.

2. GAMMA

Gamma is the rate of change of delta resulting from a change in the price of the underlying security.

Delta isn't a static number and will keep changing as the price of the underlying goes up or down. The gamma value will indicate the precise change in the delta of an option when the underlying stock price increases or decreases by 1 unit.

Here's an example to illustrate gamma.

Consider a stock 'X' with a spot price of $620. A call option of the stock X with the strike-price 620 is having a delta of 0.5 and a put option of the stock X with the strike-price of 620 is having a delta of -0.5. The gamma for both these options is 0.03. So what should be the delta values of these two options when the stock price of X goes up to $621?

In the instance of the 620 call option of X, the new delta value will become 0.53 (0.5+0.03) and in the case of the 620 put option it will become -0.47 (-0.5+0.03).

As a beginner, you need not overtly concern yourself with gamma. However, do know this – when evaluating two options exhibiting the same delta value, the one with greater gamma will have a higher risk (and also higher reward potential) because given an unfavourable move in the price of the underlying security, the option with the higher Gamma will exhibit a larger adverse change.

3. VEGA

The Vega of an option expresses the change in the price of an option for one percentage of change in the underlying security's volatility.

To understand the significance of Vega better, you need to understand volatility.

Volatility and its relevance

Understanding the concept of volatility is crucial towards trading options successfully because volatility is a key component that strongly affects options pricing at any time.

Many traders have only a vague understanding of volatility and assume volatility is just something that goes up when the market goes down, and vice versa.

This is how Investopedia, the world's leading source of financial content on the web, defines volatility - *"Volatility is a statistical measure of the dispersion of returns for a given security or market index. Volatility can either be measured by using the standard deviation or variance between returns from that same security or market index. Commonly, the higher the volatility, the riskier the security".*

Volatility, in simple words, is the measure of uncertainty in the size of the price change of the underlying security. Stock markets react negatively to uncertainty and therefore will fall when there is a greater amount of uncertainty (high volatility) and will rise when there is less uncertainty (low volatility).

Volatility is expressed as a percentage and every options trader should be aware of two types of volatility – historical and implied.

Historical Volatility

Historical volatility is the rate at which the price of the underlying security has changed in the past. This is usually determined by calculating the price movement of the underlying security over the past one year.

Accordingly, historical volatility can also be said to be the annualised standard deviation of the daily percentage price changes for the given underlying security.

Implied volatility (I.V)

The implied volatility (also commonly referred to as IV), in simplified terms, is the volatility exhibited by any particular option at present and reflects the short-term outlook an investor has on the underlying stock.

Implied volatility can be tabulated by taking the market price of an option and entering it into the Black-Scholes formula and solving back for the value of volatility.

Note: We will briefly discuss the Black-Scholes formula towards the end of this chapter.

The reason why stock traders pay attention to volatility is because they often expect a stock to revert to the levels indicated by historical volatility after short term volatility fluctuations which are denoted by implied volatility.

Say for example, a particular stock has a historical volatility of 30% and the company has announced it would be coming out with the quarterly results in the following week. Some analysts may be of the opinion that the company is likely to come out with excellent results and declare a dividend too, while other analysts could be sceptical of the results.

This level of speculation may cause the volatility of the stock to rise, let's say to 60%, before the results are declared. Traders, who buy options at that time will be buying over-priced options (because the high volatility inflates premium prices), and in all likelihood (though this isn't a hard and fast rule), once the results are out, the volatility could revert to the volatility levels the stock has displayed historically, around the 30% mark causing option prices to drop accordingly.

Many experienced traders keep an eye out for volatility spikes and then make trades to exploit such spikes.

Note: Numerous broking portals provide details of implied volatility for a given option at any time. There are also many IV calculators that you can find for free on the internet if your broker doesn't provide information on implied volatility. In my case, I use a calculator from a third-party website for determining IV before entering a trade.

4. THETA

Theta is the measure of an option's time-decay and it indicates the rate at which an option loses its time-value as it approaches its expiration date.

Theta values are always negative for a buyer because with each passing day time-value will keep decreasing. At the time of expiry, the time-value of any option (irrespective of the market, or the strike-price) will reduce to zero.

Option buyers are always in a race against time - the longer they hold any option, the greater its time-value erosion. Option sellers, on the other hand are the beneficiaries of theta-decay because theta-decay causes the premium prices of the options they short-sold to fall, making their positions more profitable by the day.

Consider this example: a stock 'X' is trading at $500 and has among its various options, a call option with a strike-price of $510 with 2 days left for expiry. The volatility of the stock is rather steady at 25% and isn't expected to change in the short term. Since there are two days left to expiry, the option has some time-value associated with it (but no intrinsic value because it is not ITM) and is trading at $1.3.

A trader, Tom, buys the mentioned call option and another trader Jerry short-sells that same call option.

Two days later, at the time of expiry, the stock price has moved only marginally up and closes at $503. Therefore, the time-premium of $1.29 erodes completely during this period, and the $510 call option expires worthless.

Accordingly, Tom, the buyer, loses the $1.3 premium he paid for that option, and Jerry, the seller, profits by $1.3.

Hope this example helped you understand how theta-decay can benefit the seller of an option and harm the buyer.

5. RHO

Rho measures the sensitivity of an option to changes in the interest rate.

For US stock market traders, Rho measures the expected change in an option's price for a 1% change in U.S. Treasury bill's risk-free rate. For Indian Stock market traders, Rho measures the expected change in an option's price for a 1% change in the Reserve Bank's Treasury bill rate.

Of all the Greeks we will be dealing with, Rho is the most predictable since the interest rates stay the same for a relatively long period (or only change by too small an amount to create any impact). Accordingly, we need to only have a general awareness of the same since Rho's influence on an option's price during the course of a regular short term options trade remains unchanged.

Few traders break their heads over the Rho value of an option and pay attention to it only when dealing with long-term options.

PS: In general, most traders stick to stock/index based options that are short term options having an expiry not more than 3 months into the future.

Using the Black-Scholes Pricing formula to determine the Greeks

The Black-Scholes Formula is the most universally accepted formula for determining the price of an option. While this formula is actually meant for calculating options that follow European style expiry (options following the American style expiry have no universally accepted formula for determining option prices), it is sometimes used informally by traders to estimate prices of American style options too, since usually, the prices determined using this model come close enough for American style options as well.

You will find numerous Black and Scholes calculators on the internet if you ever need to determine the various Greeks for an option. I personally use the Black and Scholes calculator provided by my broker Zerodha to primarily cross check the delta values for a call or put option before deciding to enter a trade such as an Iron Condor.

The image below is a screenshot of a Black and Scholes Calculator showing the various inputs required for calculating the option price and the various Greeks:

Black & Scholes Option Pricing Formula

SPOT	STRIKE	EXPIRY
365	370	2017-07-27 15:30:00
VOLATILITY (%)	INTEREST (%)	DIVIDEND
50	7	0.0

CALCULATE

CALL OPTION PREMIUM	PUT OPTION PREMIUM	CALL OPTION DELTA	PUT OPTION DELTA	OPTION GAMMA
12.42	16.42	0.475	-0.525	0.0111

CALL OPTION THETA	PUT OPTION THETA	CALL OPTION RHO	PUT OPTION RHO	OPTION VEGA
-0.539	-0.468	0.062	-0.080	0.285

In a typical Black and Scholes calculator, like the one shown above, used to determine the various Greeks and theoretical price for an option, you will need to provide the following as inputs:

1. Spot Price – This is the price at which the underlying security (stock/index) is trading in the stock market at that time.

2. Strike – This is the strike-price of the option for which the Greeks need to be calculated.

3. Expiry – This represents the number of calendar days left to expiry for that given option. In some calculators, the input required may be the number of days to expiry, whereas in others, it may be the actual calendar date of expiry (in which case, the program checks the calendar days between the expiry date and the date on which the input is provided, and does the calculation)

4. Interest Rate – This is the risk-free rate prevailing in the economy of the country in which that stock market is operating. For example, in India, this is the Reserve Bank's prevailing Treasury bill rate of 8.6% per annum. This is also a number that doesn't change very frequently and remains static during the short term.

5. Dividend – This is the dividend expected per share in the stock, if the stock is expected to yield a dividend in the expiry period. If the company is not providing a dividend during the validity period of the considered option, this value is 0.

6. Volatility – The implied volatility of the option should be ideally used for calculations here. If implied volatility is unnaturally high, the option price calculated will also reflect this.

Once input data is entered, values of the various Greeks will be tabulated and provided. This data would prove useful, along with your general outlook for that given underlying, in determining whether to go ahead with a trade.

Chapter 6: Avoiding Common Pitfalls in Trading

All successful options traders go through a learning curve before they start profiting consistently. Some of them put in an all-out effort to learn by spending countless hours reading on the topic or by watching video tutorials. Others learn at a more leisurely pace and once they get a grip of the basics, they lean more towards learning from their own experience. Irrespective of the type of learner you are, one way to cut short that learning curve is by learning from the mistakes of others.

This section lists out six of the most common mistakes made by inexperienced traders that can be easily avoided.

1. Buying Naked Options without Hedging

This is one of the most fundamental mistakes made by amateur options traders and is also one of the costliest ones that could make them go broke in no time.

Buying naked options means buying options without any protective trades to cover your investment in the event that the underlying security moves against your expectations and hurts your trade.

Here is a typical example:

A trader strongly feels a particular stock will go up in the short term and assumes he can make a huge profit by buying a few call options and therefore goes ahead with the purchase. The trader knows if the underlying stock's price were to rise as expected, the potential upside on the profits would be unlimited, whereas, if it were to go down, the maximum loss would be curtailed to just the amount invested for purchasing the call options.

In theory, the trader's assumption is right and it may so happen that this one particular trade may pay off. However, in reality, it is equally possible the stock would not move as per expectations, or may even fall. If the latter happens, the call options' prices would start falling rapidly and may never recover thereby causing major losses to that trader.

It is almost impossible to predict the short-term movement of a stock accurately every time and the trader who consistently keeps buying naked options hoping to get lucky is far more likely to lose much more than what he/she gains, in the long term.

For a person to make a profit after buying a naked option, the following things should fall in place:

1. The trader should predict the direction of underlying stock's movement correctly.

2. The directional movement of the stock price should be quick enough so that the position can be closed before its gains get overrun by time-decay.

3. The rise in the option's premium price should also compensate for any potential drop in implied volatility from the time the option was purchased.

4. The trader should exit the trade at the right time before a reversal of the stock movement happens.

Needless to say, it is impractical to expect everything to fall in place simultaneously always and that is why naked-options traders often end up losing money even when they correctly guess the direction of the underlying stock's movement.

Having said all this, many such traders often think they would fare better the next time after a botched trade and rinse and repeat their actions till they reach a point where they would have lost most of their capital and are forced to quit trading altogether.

My advice to you – never buy naked options (unless it is part of a larger strategy to hedge some position) because it's simply not worth the risk.

Note: While buying naked-options has only finite risk limited to the price of the premium paid, selling of naked-options has unlimited risk and has to be avoided too, unless hedged properly.

2. Underestimating Time-Decay

A second major mistake of inexperienced traders is underestimating time-decay.

Time-decay is your worst enemy if you are an options buyer and you don't get a chance to exit your trade quickly enough.

If you are a call options buyer, you will notice that sometimes even when your underlying stock's price is increasing every day, your call option's price still doesn't rise or even falls. Alternately, if you are a put options buyer, you sometimes notice that your put option's price doesn't increase despite a fall in the price of the underlying stock. Both these situations can be confusing to somebody new to options trading.

The above problems occur when the rate of increase/decrease in the underlying stock's price is just not enough to outstrip the rate at which the option's time-value is eroding every day.

Therefore, any trade strategy deployed by an options trader should ideally have a method of countering/minimising the effect of time-decay, or should make time-decay work in its favour, to ensure a profitable trade.

The spread based strategies (discussed in the next chapter) do exactly that.

3. Buying Options with High Implied Volatility

Buying options in times of high volatility is yet another common mistake.

During times of high volatility, option premiums can get ridiculously overpriced and at such times, if an options trader buys options, even if the stock moves sharply in line with the trader's expectation, a large drop in the implied volatility would result in the option prices falling by a fair amount, resulting in losses to the buyer.

A particular situation I remember happened the day the results of the 'Brexit' referendum came through in 2016. The Nifty index reacting to the result (like most other global indices such as the Nasdaq 100) fell very sharply and the volatility index (VIX) jumped up by over 30%. The options premium for all Nifty options had become ludicrously high that day. However, this rise in volatility was only because of the market's knee-jerk reaction to an unexpected result and just a couple of days later, the market stabilised and started rising again; the VIX fell sharply and also brought down option premium prices accordingly.

Option traders who bought options at the time VIX was high would have realised their mistake a day or two later when the option prices came down causing them substantial losses because the volatility started to get back to normal figures.

4. Not Cutting Losses on Time

There is apparently a famous saying among the folks on Wall Street - "Cut your losses short and let your winners run".

Even the most experienced options traders will make a bad trade once in a while. However, what differentiates them from a novice is that they know when to concede defeat and cut their losses. Amateurs hold on to losing trades in the hope they'll bounce back and eventually end up losing a larger chunk of their capital. The experienced traders, who know when to concede defeat, pull out early, and re-invest the capital elsewhere.

Cutting losses in time is crucial especially when you trade a directional strategy and make a wrong call. The practical thing to do is to exit a losing position if it moves against expectation and erodes more than 2-3% of your total capital.

If you are a trader who strictly uses spread-based strategies, your losses will always be far more limited whenever you make a wrong call. Nevertheless, irrespective of the strategy used, when it becomes evident that the probability of profiting from a trade is too less for whatsoever reason, it is prudent to cut losses and reinvest in a different position that has a greater chance of success rather than simply crossing your fingers or appealing to a higher power.

5. Keeping too many eggs in the same Basket

The experienced hands always know that once in a while, they will lose a trade. They also know that they should never bet too much on a single trade which could considerably erode their capital were it to go wrong.

Professionals spread their risk across different trades and keep a maximum exposure of not more than 4-5% of their total available capital in a single trade for this very reason.

Therefore, if you have a total capital of $10,000, do not enter any single trade that has a risk of losing more than $500 in the worst-case scenario. Following such a practice will ensure the occasional loss is something you can absorb without seriously eroding your cash reserve. Fail to follow this rule and you may have the misfortune of seeing many months of profits wiped out by one losing trade.

6. Using Brokers who charge High Brokerages

A penny saved is a penny earned!

When I first entered the stock market many years ago, I didn't pay much attention to the brokerage I was paying. After all, the trading services I received were from one of the largest and most reputed banks in the country and the brokerage charged by my provider wasn't very different from that of other banks that provided similar services.

Over the years, many discount brokerage firms started flourishing that charged considerably less, but I had not bothered changing my broker since I was used to the old one.

It was only when I quantified the differences that I realised having a low cost broker made a huge difference.

If you are somebody who trades in the Indian Stock markets, check the table below for a quantified break-up of how brokerage charges can eat into your earnings over a year if you choose the wrong broker. The regular broker in the table below is the bank whose trading services I had been previously using and the discount broker is the one I use now. For the record, the former is also India's third largest bank in the private sector and the latter is the most respected discount broker house in the country.

	Regular Broker	Discount Broker
Brokerage charged per options trade	₹ 300	₹ 20
Cost of entering any directional spread and exiting the position before expiry	₹ 1,200	₹ 80
Cost of entering an Iron Condor and taking it to expiry	₹ 1,200	₹ 80
Percentage of profits surrendered as brokerage for a typical Iron-Condor on Nifty index (Considering profit of ₹ 3300 for a trade with 70% winning probability)	36%	2%

Comparison of brokerages : Regular Broker versus Discount Broker

It is obvious from the table above that using a low-cost broker makes a huge difference especially when trading a strategy such as the Iron Condor (a relatively low-yield but high-probability strategy).

Also, it is not just the brokerage that burns a hole in your pocket; the annual maintenance fee is also higher for a regular broker and all these costs will make a huge difference in the long run.

Irrespective of which part of the world you trade from, always opt for a broker that provides the lowest possible brokerage because this will make a difference in the long term. Do a quantitative comparison using a table (something similar to the one I used above) and that would make it easier to decide who you should go with.

Note for India-based Traders: If you are a trader based in India or if you trade in the Indian Stock markets, I would strongly suggest using Zerodha, which has been consistently rated the best discount broker in the country. I have been using their services for the past couple of years and have found them to be particularly good. Their brokerage rates are among the best in the country, and on top of that, they provide excellent support when needed, and also maintain an exhaustive knowledge-base of articles. Lastly their trading portal is very user friendly and therefore, placing an order is quick and hassle-free.

To start a trading account with Zerodha, go the URL: **http://bit.ly/zerodhaopen**.[1]

---

[1] Disclosure: This is an affiliate link. This means that if you open an account using this link, I may be paid a minor commission, though rest assured it won't cost you anything extra. As an author, I don't make much in the way of royalties, so the affiliate commissions would be a welcome bonus to help pay the bills. Lastly, I endorse Zerodha's service because I use it myself too and have found it to be extremely satisfactory.

Chapter 7: Options Trading Strategies

Congratulations on coming this far. Even if you had no clue about options trading before starting this book, you should have learned quite a lot by now. Once you feel confident that you have a good grasp of the fundamentals, you are ready to start learning some of the best strategies for profiting from options trading.

While there are umpteen different strategies for trading options, the most consistently successful options traders will be using strategies that involve both buying and selling of options.

Do note the 'selling' of options referred above (and as part of the strategy execution throughout this chapter) is short-selling (also called writing) where the trader sells an options contract before having bought it in the first place. Such a trade position remains open till the seller squares off his position by buying back the option he sold or till the time the option expires – in which case it gets auto-settled by the exchange based on the expiry price for the underlying.

In order to allow traders to carry out short-selling or writing, brokerage firms will block an amount of money called the 'margin' – this is basically insurance money for them to cover any potential losses that could arise from writing. Since the sell price is fixed when writing an option, there is only limited profit to be gained but the trade has unlimited loss potential because there is no limit on the buy price. The required 'margin' for short-selling an option will vary from option to option and will be determined by the broker.

Spread-based Strategies

When a strategy involves the simultaneous buying and writing of an equal number of options for a given underlying, it is called a 'Spread'. This method of 'pairing' establishes an upper-limit to profits and a lower-limit to losses – both of which will be known upfront when entering the trade.

Spread based strategies are popular because they have excellent potential for giving good profits while at the same time ensuring trades are hedged (or in simple words, insured) against huge losses.

In this book, except for the last strategy (the Long Straddle), all strategies discussed are spread-based strategies.

Types of Spreads

As somebody who now understands options, you know you have to pay a premium to buy an option, and this amount appears as a debit from your trading account. Accordingly, whenever you write an option, you receive a premium that gets credited to your account. In the case of spreads, depending on the net amount paid/received for entering the trade, spreads are classified into either of the two:

1. Credit Spreads – The creation of this spread will result in a net credit into your trading account (the amount you receive for selling one leg of this spread will be greater than the amount you pay to buy the second leg of this spread).

2. Debit Spreads – The creation of this spread will result in a net debit from your trading account (the amount you pay as premium for buying one leg of the option will be greater than the amount of money you receive for selling the other leg of the option).

Spreads are also often classified into **Put Spreads** (involves the buying and selling of only put options for a given underlying) and **Call Spreads** (involves the buying and selling of only call options for a given underlying).

Lastly, the various strategies used in this book can also be classified into **directional** (profitable when the underlying moves in a particular direction only) or **non-directional** (profitable if the underlying moves in any direction).

Regarding the Case Studies in this book

As a trader, you need to know that all strategies can't be deployed at all times. Choosing the right strategy and the right stock/index to trade at the right time has a lot to do with eventual success/failure.

There is one case study each that has been included at the end of each strategy discussed in this book.

The objective of providing a detailed case-study against each strategy is to illustrate the rationale behind choosing a particular stock/index to trade at that time and to show how that trade progressed till it was closed. Seeing strategies in action as part of a case study will enhance your learning on how to approach trading options.

Note: The case studies listed in this book are based on trades carried out in India's National Stock Exchange (commonly called the NSE), which is the 12th largest stock exchange in the world, and is among the most prominent stock exchanges in Asia. Accordingly, the trades have been undertaken in Indian Rupees (denoted by ₹).

However, all concepts and strategies apply universally. Therefore, irrespective of whether you trade on the NYSE, FTSE, or the Hang Seng, the knowledge you acquire here will be equally useful and applicable.

The Strategies Workbook

There is an MS Excel workbook that is provided as a downloadable bonus along with this book that you will find quite handy when you are ready to start trading options.

You will find this workbook especially useful if you are somebody like me who uses a cost-effective no-frills broker that provides only a minimalistic trading portal.

This workbook is split into worksheets and each worksheet corresponds to one of the six strategies from this book.

The worksheets are pre-populated with details you will come across in individual case studies – this will help you understand the usage of the worksheets with ease.

Instructions are also embedded in these individual worksheets in the form of comments.

Use these worksheets before entering a trade so that even before execution, you know what your maximum exposure would be, and what could be your maximum gain from that trade. The worksheets for each strategy will also plot your Profit/Loss Payoff chart, and help you calculate the profit or loss for that options trade, for a given price of the underlying stock/index, at expiry time.

This workbook is meant to save you a lot of time by automating manual work and will help you make decisions faster.

You can download the Strategies Workbook from the following URL:

http://bit.ly/UltimateOptionsWorkbook

Important Note: The URL provided above is case-sensitive and hence you need to enter the given URL in your browser exactly as provided above to access the Strategies Workbook.

Strategy 1: The Bull Put Spread

The Bull Put Spread is a directional strategy that can be used when a stock has shown signs of having reached its support level from where it is unlikely to fall further. At this stage, the stock is either trading flat (hardly any movement in either direction) or has started rising again.

The Bull Put Spread is a type of credit spread. There are two 'legs' in this trade and a trader will receive a net credit on entering this trade.

How to Execute this Strategy

For creating a Bull Put Spread you need to do the following:

Step 1: Select a stock/index that fits the criteria for trading this strategy based on your short or medium term outlook for the stock/index.

Step 2: Sell one OTM put option of this stock/index.

Step 3: Buy one OTM put option with the same expiry-date and of the same underlying stock/index as that of the put option in Step 2, but with a lower strike-price.

Once the above steps are complete, monitor your position continuously and square off (close) both the options back-to-back once the trade is significantly in profit. Alternately, you can also hold on to the trade until expiry of the options for retaining maximum profit – do this only if the stock is not under any threat of falling below the strike-price of the higher-strike put option before the expiry.

Tip: Sell an OTM put option with a delta value between -0.25 to -0.2 with at least a month left to expiry and then buy an OTM put option that is 1 or 2 strikes lower. This way you retain a high probability of success (75% - 80%) while also collecting a substantial net premium.

When to Use this Strategy

Trade this spread when you believe the underlying stock/index has reached a strong support level with little chances of going down much further from that level before expiry time (of the options you intend to trade in).

A good time to enter this trade is when the underlying stock/index has undergone some expected correction or profit booking. Say for example a fundamentally strong stock underwent a fair correction (declined by 5% or so) and then started showing signs of stability at lower levels, with buying volumes and net buyers steadily increasing which indicates the stock is far more likely to go up than down. Alternately, you can trade this when a stock is gradually climbing up and is very unlikely to fall in the near-term.

It is preferable to trade options with historically low-volatility stocks in this strategy. Since this is a credit spread strategy that exploits time-decay, a price-fall in low-volatility stocks is likely to be only marginal and therefore unlikely to overcome the time-decay of the options - this keeps the trade profitable even when the stock moves against expectations. Nevertheless, this isn't a hard and fast rule and this strategy can be used for higher-volatility stocks too, if the right opportunity comes by (as illustrated in the case study to follow).

Profit and Loss Potential

The chart that follows shows a typical profit and loss payoff chart for a Bull Put Spread.

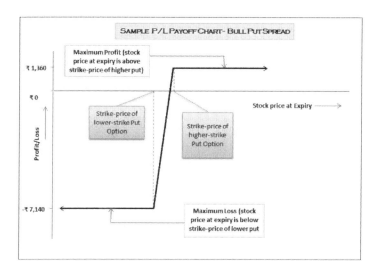

[*Note: Numbers used in the chart above are indicative only.*]

If you correlate the chart above with the execution steps outlined in the earlier section, the higher-strike put option price in the chart corresponds to the OTM put option sold in Step 2 and the lower-strike put option price in the chart corresponds to the deep OTM put option bought in Step 3.

The chart also shows the maximum profit you can make on a Bull Put Spread is when at the time of expiry, the stock price is trading above the strike-price of the higher put option.

Maximum Profit = (Premium received for selling higher-strike put option – Premium paid for buying lower-strike put option) x Lot size.

The maximum loss you can incur on a Bull Put Spread is when, at the time of expiry, the stock price falls below the strike-price of the lower-strike put option.

Maximum Loss = [(Difference of the two strike-prices) – (Net premium received)] x Lot Size.

Note: Brokerages, as applicable, need to be factored in to get a more accurate profit/loss calculation.

Advantages v/s Disadvantages

The Bull Put Spread's biggest advantage is that it makes time-decay (the worst enemy of option buyers) work in your favour. Even if the underlying stock doesn't move up after hitting the support level and stays stagnant (or even falls marginally), you still get to gain with each passing day because of time-decay.

Also, if traded in times of high volatility, any subsequent volatility drop will also act as a catalyst in making the trade become profitable faster.

The one notable disadvantage of this strategy is that the maximum profit you can gain is much less than the potential loss you could incur, if the underlying stock/index falls significantly against expectations and the position gets into losses.

Case Study of a Bull Put Spread Trade

The following is a study of an actual trade that was executed successfully using this strategy.

Trade Entry Date: 27th of April 2017

Underlying Stock: Biocon Limited

Exchange: National Stock Exchange (NSE), India.

Background of the traded Stock: Biocon is a pharmaceutical company that has been steadily growing and its stock valuation had surged over 300% in a little over 2 years because of strong and steady revenue and profit growth. It is also one of the strong mid-cap stocks in the Pharmaceutical sector traded on the NSE.

The annual results of the company were due on the 27th of April 2017 and the stock started showing high volatility two days prior to this date. The stock had also surged by approximately 9% following a news announcement about an upcoming bonus issue and later corrected to a price 2.5% lower than the high it had touched following that surge. The market analysts were having high expectations from the upcoming results, and historically, the company's share prices almost always rose after the announcement of quarterly or annual results.

Reasons for entering trade: Biocon's options were trading, on the morning of the expiry date, with a high implied volatility (IV) of around 95% (very high when compared with the annual volatility of the stock that was only around 45%) and the high implied volatility caused premium prices of all Biocon options to rise substantially, including those OTM options that were due to expire the same day - the 27th of April.

In the opening hour of trade on 27th of April 2017, the stock was trading around the 1140 mark – this was 25 points below the previous day's high. Given the high expectations from the stock, it seemed unlikely to fall much further; also at every price-dip, investors were buying the stock in anticipation of good results.

Historically, Biocon published results only late in the day well after trading hours and therefore, even a negative reaction to an unlikely bad result would to be felt only the next day (28th of April) and not on the same day.

Therefore, to sum up the context of the trade, here was a stock with a low probability of falling further during the course of the day. Its option premiums were expensive because of high implied volatility and its April series of options were due for expiry later in the same day.

A option writer who sold slightly OTM put options with April month's expiry had a good chance of retaining most/all of the premium he/she received by end of day.

Therefore, the conditions looked ideal for a short-term Bull Put trade for which a small profit could be booked within the same day.

Steps followed for executing the trade

The Bull Put Spread was executed using options of Biocon Limited, as follows:

Step 1: Determine options with optimum strike-prices to trade.

The first thing to do was to determine a put option to sell that had a delta of no more than -0.25. The delta of -0.25 meant the trade had the right balance of probability and potential profit and implied there was only a 25% chance of the option ending ITM at expiry, or in other words, it indicated a 75% chance of success with a decent amount of premium to be collected.

Using a standard Black and Scholes calculator, the Biocon put option with a strike-price of 1100 and a delta of -22.7 was chosen to be written (short-sold).

Step 2: Sell OTM put option.

The Biocon 1100 put option with the 27th of April expiry (same day expiry) was sold for ₹4.70.

Step 3: Buy a lower-strike OTM put option of the same stock with same expiry date.

The Biocon 1080 put option with 27th of April expiry was bought for ₹1.75 to complete the second leg of the trade.

The following table shows a summary of key details of the trade that was executed:

Summary Table		
Stock or Index Traded	Biocon Ltd.	
Lot size for option	600	
Option 1	Strike Price	1100
Higher-strike OTM Put : Sell	Premium Received	₹ 4.70
Option 2	Strike Price	1080
Lower-strike OTM Put : Buy	Premium Paid	₹ 1.75
Potential Max Profit		₹ 1,770
Potential Max Loss		-₹ 10,230
Condition for meeting max profit	Stock price at expiry >=	1,100
Condition for meeting max loss	Stock price at expiry <=	1,080
Break-even	Stock Price at expiry =	1,097.05

The tabulation shows the maximum profit that could be attained if the Biocon stock stayed above 1100. At the end of the day it was ₹1,770.

The maximum loss that could be incurred in the unlikely event the stock fell below the lower-strike was ₹ 10,230.

The break-even point (above which the trade would remain profitable) was 1097.05 (higher strike-price – the net premium received) and statistically speaking, the delta values of the traded options suggested a less than a 20% chance of the trade ending in a loss.

The profit/loss payoff diagram below shows the profit and loss plotted against five different expiry prices for the Biocon stock for the trade that was entered into.

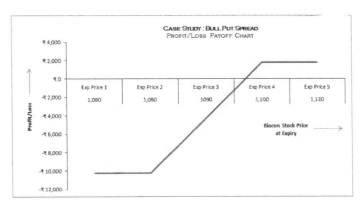

Result of the Trade

Despite the Biocon stock showing some intraday fluctuation, it eventually ended the day at 1123. Therefore, both the options expired worthless as OTM options that resulted in an overall profit for the trade.

The table on the next page shows the various details of the trade at closure (shaded prices indicate the price-points at entry).

Entry Date	Exit Date	No. Trading Days	Stock Price at Entry	Options Traded	Lot size	Option Strike Price	Option Buy Price	Cost Price per Lot	Option Sell Price	Sell Price per Lot	P/L per Trade Leg	Stock Price at Exit	Overall P/L
27-Apr	27-Apr	1	1,140	Biocon PE	600	1,100	₹0.00	₹0.00	₹4.70	₹2,820.00	₹2,820.00	1,123	₹1,770
				Biocon PE		1,080	₹1.75	₹1,050.00	₹0.00	₹0.00	-₹1,050.00		

The trade yielded a profit of ₹1770. This was also the maximum potential profit and was equal to the net premium received on entering the trade. Since both the options expired at ₹0.0, maximum returns were realised.

Return on Investment (ROI)

The ratio of the net profit (or loss) to the sum invested in the trade will give the return-on-investment, which in other words is percentage of profit earned in this trade.

A sum of ₹86,000 was blocked by the broker as margin for selling the 1100 Biocon put option that was sold for a total sum of ₹2820 (premium of ₹4.7 x lot size of 600) and a total sum of ₹1050 (premium of ₹1.75 x lot size of 600) was paid for purchasing the lower-strike put option.

Therefore the total investment in this trade was ₹86,000 + ₹1050 = ₹87,050. The net profit was ₹1770, as mentioned earlier.

A quick tabulation shows the profit ratio as 0.02, or in other terms the trade yielded a return of 2% - fair returns given the holding time for that trade was barely 6 hours.

Note: The brokerages incurred were negligible, and hence, were not included in calculations.

Worksheet for Bull Put Spread

The Bull Put Spread worksheet is the second worksheet in the Strategies Workbook and you can use it to paper-trade or to check profit/loss potential before you execute this strategy.

Strategy 2: The Bear Call Spread

The Bear Call spread is a directional strategy that is used when a trader believes the underlying stock /index has reached its upper resistance level and is unlikely to go much further up at this point and would likely stay flat (unchanged) or undergo correction. This strategy is effectively the opposite of the previous strategy we went through – the Bull Put Spread.

Like the previous strategy discussed, the Bear Call Spread is also a type of credit spread. In other words, the premium you receive while selling one leg of this trade is greater than the premium you pay for buying the second leg of this trade and therefore you receive a net credit into your account when you enter the position.

How to Execute this Strategy

For creating a Bear Call Spread, you need to do the following:

Step 1: Select a stock/index that fits the criteria for trading this strategy based on your short or medium term outlook for the stock/index.

Step 2: Sell an OTM call option of the selected stock/index.

Step 3: Buy an OTM call option with the same expiry date and of the same underlying as that of the ATM call option but with a higher strike-price.

Monitor your position every day. Exit your position once your position is considerably in profit (> 50% of max profit) or alternately, if there's no risk of a reversal that will take the stock price beyond the strike-price of the sold call option, wait till expiry and pocket maximum profit.

Tip: Sell an OTM call option having a delta value between 0.25 and 0.2 and having at least a month left for expiry and then buy an OTM call option having 2 strikes greater than the sold call option. This ensures you retain a high (75-80%) probability of success and also receive substantial premium.

When to Use this Strategy

You can enter a Bear Call Spread when you have substantial reason to believe that the underlying stock/index is unlikely to rise in the near-term and would most probably decline from its current price or stagnate. For example: the stock of a company from which there were huge market expectations just posted results that were far below market expectations (such as a loss or a decline in profits or net sales). Alternately, if you are trading in index options and if the index has hit a major resistance level, it would be a good time to trade a Bear Call Spread.

Do not enter this trade when the stock/index is volatile and likely to rise substantially in the short term.

Profit and Loss Potential

The chart on the next page shows a typical payoff chart for a Bear Call Spread.

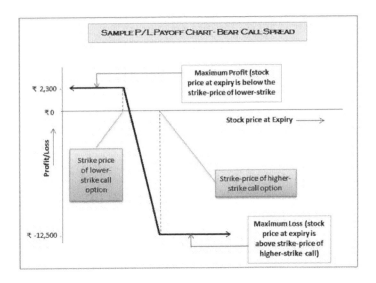

[Note: Numbers used in the chart above are indicative only.]

If you correlate the chart above with the execution steps outlined in the earlier section, the strike-price of the lower-strike call option in the chart corresponds to the OTM call option sold in Step 2 and the strike-price of the higher-strike call option in the chart corresponds to the OTM call option bought in Step 3.

The maximum profit you can make on the Bear Call Spread is when at the time of expiry, the stock price is trading below the strike-price of the call option (with the lower strike-price) that was sold.

Maximum Profit = (Premium received for selling lower-strike call option – Premium paid for purchasing higher-strike call option) x Lot size.

The maximum loss you can incur on this spread is when at the time of expiry the stock price is trading above the strike-price call option you bought (with the higher strike-price).

Maximum Loss = [(Higher strike-price – Lower strike-price) x Lot size] – Net premium received.

Note: Brokerages, as applicable, need to be factored in to get a more accurate profit/loss calculation.

Advantages v/s Disadvantages

As is the case with the Bull Put Spread, the biggest advantage of the Bear Call Spread is that it makes time-decay work in your favour and as long as the stock stays below the lower strike-price by the time of expiry, you will get to keep the entire net credit you received while entering the position.

The disadvantage of this position is that if the stock makes a sharp movement against expectations, the maximum loss that can be incurred will be much greater than the maximum profit that could've been gained.

Case Study of a Bear Call Spread Trade

The following is a study of an actual trade that was executed successfully using this strategy.

Trade Entry Date: 26th of May 2017

Underlying Index: Nifty 50 (Benchmark Index of the NSE, India).

Exchange: National Stock Exchange (NSE), India.

Background of the traded Index: The Nifty 50 is the benchmark index of India's NSE. It is a diversified 50 stock index and accounts for 12 sectors of the Indian economy. It has historically shown a high level of stability with an average daily volatility of only about 0.53%.

Reasons for entering trade: The market had gone through an extended bull run for over a month and showed signs of running out of steam. The Nifty index was showing signs of having encountered stiff resistance when it touched the 9500 mark and didn't look likely to cross that barrier in the short term. Hence, it seemed a good opportunity to create a Bear Call Spread at that point expecting some stagnation at the 9500 mark or a correction to lower levels, before moving forward.

Steps followed for executing the trade

The Bear Call Spread was executed using the options of Nifty as follows:

Step 1: Determine options with optimum strike-prices to trade.

Since the resistance level for the index was found to be at the 9500 mark, it was decided to sell an OTM option which was four strikes away from the spot price of Nifty, which was at that time trading at 9500. Therefore, the 9700 Nifty call option with expiry a month away (in June) was selected to be written, and to complete the second leg of the trade, the 9900 Nifty Call was also selected.

Note: As done with the Bull Put Spread, a standard Black and Scholes calculator was used to check the deltas of these options and the delta of the lower-strike call was found to be 0.31. This implied a 31% chance of the 9700 Nifty Call becoming ITM by expiry time. The 9700 strike, therefore, had a slightly higher risk than what is recommended for credit based strategies, but since the Nifty index had shown signs of having peaked, it was a risk worth taking.

Step 2: Sell OTM call option

The Nifty 9700 call option with June 29th Expiry was written for ₹46.00 to complete the first leg of the trade.

Step 3: Buy OTM call option

The Nifty 9900 call option with June 29th Expiry was bought for ₹9.80 and this completed the second leg of the trade.

The following table shows a summary of the key details of the trade that was executed:

Summary Table		
Stock or Index Traded	Nifty	
Lot size for each option	75	
Option 1	Strike Price	9700
Lower-strike Call Option - Sell	Premium Received	₹ 46.00
Option 2	Strike Price	9900
Higher-strike Call Option - Buy	Premium Paid	₹ 9.80
Max Profit		₹ 2,715
Max Loss		₹ -12,285
Condition for maximum profit	Index price of underlying at time of expiry <	9700
Condition for maximum loss	Index Price at time of expiry > 9900	
Break-even	Index at time of Expiry = 9,736.20	

The table shows the maximum profit of ₹2,715 could be made, if the Nifty Index, at the time of expiry, stayed at 9700 or below.

The maximum loss of ₹12,285 would be incurred in the event the Nifty index, at the time of expiry, had crossed 9900.

The break-even point is 9736.2 (lower strike-price + the net premium received) and as long as the index at the time of expiry is above this point, the trade would result in a profit.

(Note: Net premium received = ₹46 – ₹9.8 = ₹36.2)

The profit/loss payoff diagram below shows the profit and loss plotted against five different expiry prices for the index.

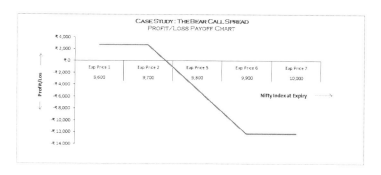

Result of the Trade:

Contrary to expectations, in the week that followed, the Nifty Index did not move down from 9500 and broke the resistance level and went all the way up to 9700 before slowing down and trading in the 9600-9670 range. Within a week the 9700 call that was sold for ₹46 had touched ₹80 before the premium came down to around ₹70!

The trade position was in a net loss for the next two weeks because of this development. However, the Nifty index couldn't sustain over 9700 and within 3 weeks, the inherent advantage of the Bear Call Spread came into the picture and time-decay brought considerable erosion to the two options. On the 21st of June, when the Nifty came down by 25 points during opening, and was trading around the 9620 mark, the position was exited, for a profit.

Final details of the trade at the time of closure are shown in the table below:

Entry Date	Exit Date	No. Trading Days	Index Price at Entry	Options Traded	Lot size	Option Strike Price	Option Buy Price	Cost Price per Lot	Option Sell Price	Sell Price per Lot	P/L per Trade Leg	Index Price at Exit	Overall P/L
26-May	21-Jun	15	9,500	Nifty CE	75	1,100	₹ 23.75	₹ 1,781.25	₹ 46.00	₹ 3,450.00	₹ 1,668.75	9,625	₹ 1,087.50
				Nifty CE		1,080	₹ 9.80	₹ 735.00	₹ 2.05	₹ 153.75	-₹ 581.25		

The shaded data cells show the prices at entry for the two options.

You can see that the index price had risen from 9500 to 9625 at the time the trade was exited. However, the time-decay over the 3 week duration overran the appreciation in the index price and since the Bear Call Spread is a credit spread that benefits from theta- decay, the trade still resulted in a profit.

The trade was closed for an overall profit of ₹1087.50 on the 21st of June.

While there was a possibility of earning further profit by carrying the trade till the expiry date on the 29th of June, since there was also heightened probability of encountering a loss due to the unexpected run-up, it was exited early.

Return on Investment (ROI)

The ratio of the net profit (or loss) to the sum invested in the trade will give the ROI in this trade.

A sum of approximately ₹40,000 was blocked by the broker as margin for selling the 9700 call option that was sold for ₹46 and a total sum of ₹735 (premium of ₹9.8 x lot size of 75) was paid for purchasing the higher-strike call option. Therefore, the total investment in this trade was ₹40,000 + ₹735 = ₹40,735.

The net profit was ₹1087.5 as shown in the previous section. Therefore, dividing the net profit by total investment shows the profit ratio as 0.27, or in other terms the trade still yielded a return of 2.7% in 3 weeks - this is despite the underlying Nifty index moving against expectations.

Note: Brokerages incurred were negligible and hence not included in the calculations above.

Worksheet for the Bear Call Spread

The Bear Call Spread worksheet is the third worksheet in the Strategies Workbook and you can use it to paper-trade or to check profit/loss potential before you execute this strategy.

Strategy 3: The Iron Condor

The Iron Condor is a non-directional strategy that yields limited profit but has a high probability of success when traded diligently. In an Iron Condor trade, irrespective of which direction the underlying stock or index moves, the trader will profit as long as the movement stays within the defined boundaries, at the time of expiry.

Of all strategies discussed in this book, this is the strategy that has the highest potential to consistently give profits with the least amount of risk.

The Iron Condor is traded on stocks/indices with historically low volatility. It is also a credit spread strategy that can be viewed as a combination of the previous two strategies discussed – the Bull Put Spread and the Bear Call Spread.

The Iron Condor is the evergreen strategy used by stock traders for stable stocks. As a trader, if you have the luxury to choose just one strategy to trade, you should choose the Iron Condor because it is the one trade that can help build wealth over a long term given its high likelihood of success.

How to Execute this Strategy

There are four legs in the Iron Condor trade. To create an Iron Condor spread, you need to do the following:

Step 1: Identify an optimum stock/index that fits the criteria for trading this strategy.

Step 2: Sell one deep-OTM put option of the selected stock/index.

Step 3: Buy one OTM put option with the same expiry date and with the same underlying as that of the option sold in Step 1, but with a lower strike-price.

Step 4: Sell a deep OTM call option with the same expiry date and with the same underlying as that of the two put options in Steps 1 and 2.

Step 5: Buy an OTM call option with the same expiry date and of the same underlying as that of the afore-mentioned call option but with a higher strike-price.

Note: The difference between the strike-prices of the two put options should be the same as the difference between the strikes of the two call options to create the Iron Condor.

Monitor your position from time to time. Exit your position once your position is considerably in profit (> 50% of max profit). Alternately, if the stock or index continues to show no sign of strong movement in any particular direction, hold on till expiry. If there is a case for any strong directional movement of the underlying, exit the trade by closing all positions and re-enter only after the stock has stabilised.

Tip: Sell an OTM put option with a delta value of about -0.15 with at least a month left to expiry and an OTM call option with a delta of about 0.15. This gives you approximately a 70% chance of successfully closing the Iron Condor for maximum profit. Also, when buying the protective put and call options mentioned in step 3 and step 5, ensure they are 2 strikes away so that you get a chance to earn decent profits. The two protective options are more than 95% likely to expire worthless (which is our default expectation), but we buy them anyway since they will protect our position against any unexpected 'black-swan' events and will limit losses in the case of such an event.

When to Use this Strategy

Trade an Iron Condor when a stock/index is showing low volatility, or in other words, is showing only slow movement, or if the stock/index is consistently moving in a well-defined range. Generally, index-based options are more suited for executing an Iron Condor than stock-based options since indexes are generally less volatile than individual stocks.

In a stable market, Iron Condors are the safest bet for a winning trade.

Profit and Loss Potential

The chart below shows a typical profit and loss payoff chart for an Iron Condor at the time of expiry.

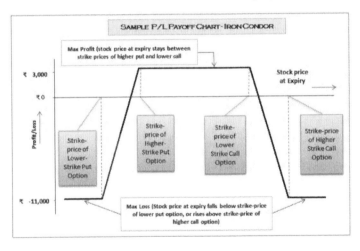

[Note: Numbers used in the chart above are indicative only.]

If you correlate the chart above with the execution steps in the earlier section, the higher-strike put option strike-price in the chart corresponds to the OTM put option sold in Step 2 and the lower-strike put option strike-price in the chart corresponds to the deep OTM put option bought in Step 3. Likewise, the lower-strike call option strike-price in the chart corresponds to the OTM call option sold in Step 4 and the higher-strike call option strike-price in the chart corresponds to the OTM call option bought in Step 5.

The maximum profit you can make on an Iron Condor is when at the time of expiry, the stock price is trading between the strike-price of the lower call option and the higher put option.

Maximum Profit = (Net premium received after entering the four legs of the trade) x Lot size.

The maximum loss you can incur on the Iron Condor is when, at the time of expiry, the stock price is either above the strike-price of the higher call option, or below the strike-price of the lower put option.

Maximum Loss = [Difference between the strike-prices of either the two call options **or** the difference between strike-prices of the two put options x Lot size] – Net premium received.

Note: Brokerages, as applicable, need to be factored in to get a more accurate profit/loss calculation.

Advantages v/s Disadvantages

The biggest advantage of the Iron Condor is that it is a neutral position and it is highly likely to give a profit when executed correctly irrespective of which direction the underlying stock/index moves. Another advantage is that since the Iron Condor is a net credit strategy, it will leverage time-decay.

A primary disadvantage of the Iron Condor is that the returns you get from it are relatively less when compared with a directional strategy. Also, the maximum loss that can be incurred would be substantially more than the maximum profit that can be gained from a position. Nevertheless, statistically speaking, the probability of a win is far more than that of a loss and that is what makes this a preferred strategy.

Case Study of an Iron Condor Trade

This following example shows how an options trader successfully traded an Iron Condor and closed it for a profit.

Trade Entry Date: 17th of April 2017

Underlying Index: Nifty 50 (Benchmark Index of the NSE, India).

Exchange: National Stock Exchange (NSE), India.

Background of the traded Index: The Nifty 50 is the benchmark index of India's NSE. It is a diversified 50 stock index and accounts for 12 sectors of the Indian economy. It has traditionally shown a high level of stability with a mean daily volatility of only about 0.53%.

Reasons for entering trade: The Nifty index had touched its 52-week high a couple of weeks earlier and had seen some profit booking. It then had been trading in a narrow range showing strong support around 9100 and strong resistance around the 9300 mark. There were no major triggers expected in the near-term that would cause a significant spike or drop. Historically, Nifty has seldom moved more than +/- 3% on an average any month, and therefore it was unlikely the index would rise over 9500 or fall below 8900 within the chosen expiry period. The conditions looked ideal for setting up an Iron Condor.

Steps followed for executing the trade

These were the steps undertaken to execute the trade.

Step 1: Select the right options to trade for the chosen stock/index.

The following criteria were taken into consideration to select the options to trade as part of the Iron Condor:

i. All options should have a minimum of 30 days to expiry so that sufficient premium could be collected – this resulted in selecting monthly options with the 25th of May expiry (38 calendar days to expiry)

ii. The trade should have a high probability of success (around 70%) – to ensure this, the 8900 Nifty put option and 9500 call option were chosen to be written. Since the Nifty index had only recently corrected and was around the 9150 mark, the strikes chosen gave more room for movement on the call side since the index had greater chance moving up rather than down at that point.

Note: A standard Black and Scholes calculator was used to determine the deltas for various strike-prices.

Step 2: Sell one deep OTM put option.

The Nifty 8900 put option with May Expiry was sold for ₹45.25.

Step 3: Buy one OTM put option with a lower strike-price than the sold option.

The Nifty 8700 put option with May Expiry was bought at ₹19.70.

Step 4: Sell a deep OTM call option

The Nifty 9500 call option with May Expiry was sold for ₹23.

Step 5: Buy an OTM call option

The Nifty 9700 call option with May Expiry was bought at ₹4.85.

A summary of the Iron Condor position taken and the key indicators are shown in the table below:

Summary Table		
Stock or Index Traded	Nifty	
Lot size for each option	75	
Option 1	Strike Price	8900
Higher-strike Put Option - Sell	Premium Received	₹ 45.25
Option 2	Strike Price	8700
Lower-strike Put Option - Buy	Premium Paid	₹ 19.70
Option 3	Strike Price	9500
Lower-strike Call Option - Sell	Premium Received	₹ 23.00
Option 4	Strike Price	9700
Higher-strike Call Option - Buy	Premium Paid	₹ 4.85
Max Profit		₹ 3,278
Max Loss		₹ -11,723
Condition for meeting max profit	Stock price at time of expiry is between strike-prices of the two sold options	
Condition for meeting max loss	Stock Price at time of expiry > Strike price of Higher-Strike Call or Stock Price at time of expiry < Strike price of Lower-Strike Put	
Upper Break-even Price at Expiry	9,543.70	
Lower Break-even Price at Expiry	8,856.30	

Based on the various prices at which individual legs of the position was entered, the potential maximum profit was tabulated and found to be ₹3,278 (this is the net premium received) and the potential maximum loss that could be incurred in the case of an unforeseen event was tabulated and found to be ₹11,723 (difference of strike-prices on either side less the net premium received).

Note: The net premium received is the sum of premiums received minus the premiums paid. The net premium received is therefore (₹45.25 + ₹23) – (₹19.7 + ₹4.5) = ₹43.7

The Iron Condor position has two break-even points –the upper break-even price was ₹9543.7 (Strike-price of sold call option + the net premium received) and the lower break-even price was ₹8,856.3 (Strike-price of sold put option – the net premium received)

The profit/loss payoff diagram below shows the profit and loss plotted against different expiry prices for the Nifty index for this trade.

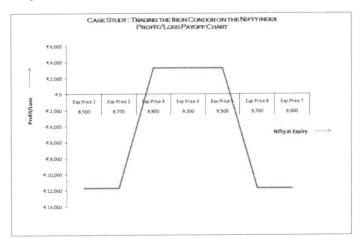

Result of the Trade:

The position was held for 3 weeks and then closed. Though the trader still had 2 weeks left for expiry of these options, he decided to exit early because he wanted to free capital to enter a different trade. Secondly, the Nifty index had also climbed an all-time high and there was a possibility that the momentum could carry it further forward before it cooled off thereby reducing the profit from this trade.

The table below shows the details of the prices at which the individual legs of the Iron Condortrade were exited on 10th of May (shaded prices indicate the price-points at entry).

Entry Date	Exit Date	No. Trading Days	Index Price at Entry	Options Traded	Lot size	Option Strike Price	Option Buy Price	Cost Price per Lot	Option Sell Price	Sell Price per Lot	P/L per Trade Leg	Index Price at Exit	Overall P/L
17-Apr	10-May	23	9,140	Nifty 8700 PE	75	1,100	₹19.70	₹1,477.50	₹2.50	₹187.50	-₹1,290.00	9,392	₹1,054
				Nifty 8900 PE		1,080	₹5.20	₹390.00	₹45.25	₹3,393.75	₹3,003.75		
17-Apr	10-May	23		Nifty 9700 CE		1,100	₹29.45	₹2,208.75	₹23.00	₹1,725.00	-₹483.75		
				Nifty 9900 CE		1,080	₹4.85	₹363.75	₹2.50	₹187.50	-₹176.25		

Do note that despite the Nifty index having gained 250 points in the 3 week period, the IronCondor trade still yielded a profit of almost 30% of the maximum potential profit because of time-decay and at the time of exit, had yielded a net profit of ₹1,024.

Return on Investment (ROI)

The ratio of the net profit (or loss) to the sum invested in the trade will give the profit percentage return for this trade, or in other words, the ROI.

An approximate sum of ₹83,000 was blocked by the broker as the total margin for writing the 8900 put option and the 9500 call option. Additionally, a total premium of ₹1841 (rounded off) was paid for purchasing the 8700 Nifty put option and the Nifty 9700 call option. Therefore the total investment in this trade was the blocked margin of ₹83,000 + premium paid ₹1841.

The profit percentage will therefore be the ratio of net profit (₹1054) to the total investment and a quick tabulation will show that this is approximately 1.25%

Note: The above trade is not typical of every Iron Condor trade since the index moved more than expected in the given period. On an average a trade similar to the above one on the Nifty Index gives a return of between 3 and 3.5% over a month and such gains, when viewed in the context of a longer term gives a cumulative gain of over 30% in a calendar year when traded once every month.

Worksheet for the Iron Condor

The Iron Condor worksheet is the fourth worksheet in the Strategies Workbook and you can use it to paper-trade or to check profit/loss potential before you execute this strategy.

Strategy 4: The Bull Call Spread

The Bull Call Spread is a directional strategy that that can be deployed when a trader has a positive outlook on the underlying stock/index and expects it to rise moderately in the short term.

As it is for any other spread based strategy, both the potential profits and potential losses are capped in the Bull Call Spread. However, the distinct advantage of the Bull Call Spread is that maximum profit that can be gained from this kind of spread exceeds the maximum loss that could be incurred, by a fair margin.

Unlike the previous three strategies discussed, the Bull Call Spread is a debit spread and hence you will need to pay a net debit to enter into the position.

The Bull Call Spread and the Bear Put Spread (discussed next) are the two directional strategies that can give a high percentage of returns because these spreads can be used to capitalise directional momentum while keeping risk relatively low.

How to Execute this Strategy

Step 1: Identify an optimum stock/index that fits the criteria for trading this strategy.

Step 2: Buy one slightly OTM call option.

Step 3: Sell one OTM call option that has a strike-price 1 or 2 strikes higher than the option bought in Step 1, and with the same expiry date and of the same underlying stock/index.

Monitor your position periodically and close both positions once the trade has yielded significant profits (profit reaches 30-40% of maximum potential profit).

When to Use this Strategy

Trade the Bull Call Spread when the market has positive outlook on the stock following some positive development such as a good earnings result, or a strategic move by the company that could increase growth.

A Bull Call Spread can also be traded on stocks that have been overcorrected and have started showing strong signs of a reversal.

Note: Since this is a debit spread strategy, time-decay will work against the position even though decay will be much slower when compared with a naked long call position. Typically, it wouldn't be advisable to hold this spread for more than a couple of weeks, unless the position is continuously gaining at the end of two weeks with a lot more expected upside. If the stock is showing no momentum for more than two weeks, it would be prudent to exit the position at small losses and free the capital for other trades rather than hoping for a turnaround and losing the maximum amount at risk.

Profit and Loss Potential

The chart on the next page shows a typical profit and loss payoff chart for a Bull Call Spread.

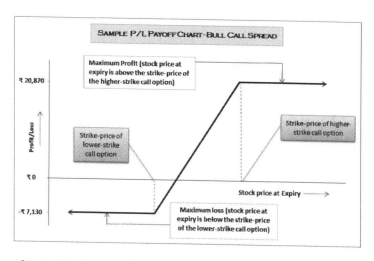

[Note: Numbers used in the chart above are indicative only.]

If you correlate the chart above with the execution steps in the earlier section, the strike-price of the lower-strike call option corresponds to the strike-price of the call option bought in Step 2 and the strike-price of the higher-strike call option corresponds to the strike-price of the call option sold in Step 3.

As illustrated in the chart above, maximum profit can be made on a Bull Call Spread when at the time of expiry the stock is trading above the strike-price of the higher-strike call option.

Maximum Profit = [(Difference of the two strike-prices of the call options) – (Net premium paid to enter the position)] x Lot size.

Maximum Loss is incurred on the Bull Call Spread when the price of the stock at expiry is below the strike-price of the lower-strike call option.

Maximum Loss = (Net premium paid to enter position) x Lot size.

Net Premium = Premium paid for lower-strike call option – Premium received for higher-strike call option.

Note: Brokerages, as applicable, need to be factored in to get a more accurate profit/loss calculation.

Example: A stock X was trading at 500 when a Bull Call Spread was traded using the 520 call option of Stock X and the 540 call option of Stock X, both options expiring the same month. If stock X rises and stays above 540 at the time of expiry of the options, maximum profit will be gained. On the contrary, if stock X stays below 520 at the time of expiry of these options, maximum loss will be incurred.

Advantages v/s Disadvantages

The primary advantage of this trade is that it has a very good reward to risk ratio and a moderate up move by the stock can result in decent profits.

You can also increase the profit potential of this spread by widening the spread (increasing the strike-prices between the two options) or you can choose to reduce the risk further by decreasing the spread (decreasing the number of strike-prices between the two options)

The notable disadvantage of this spread is that time-decay works against the position and despite the limited loss potential, if the stock stays stagnant for too long, the position will end in a loss.

Case Study of a Bull Call Spread Trade

This case study is to illustrate how a Bull Call Spread was executed and closed successfully.

Trade entry Date: 30th of May 2017

Underlying Stock: Tech Mahindra Limited

Exchange: National Stock Exchange (NSE), India.

Background of the traded Stock: Tech Mahindra Limited is India's 3rd largest Information Technology organisation with over 110,000 employees and a market turnover of USD 4Billion. The company has clients all over the globe, mostly global telecommunications operators.

Reasons for entering trade: Tech Mahindra's earnings for the 4th quarter of the 2016-2017 financial year failed to live up to the expectations of various brokerage firms and showed a decline in EBIDTA, though revenue growth was on par with expectations.

The stock, reacting to the earnings news, fell by over 17%, in a single day- which was viewed as overcorrection, given that the company was fundamentally still sound, and profitable. Besides, the stock had already undergone a recent correction in the preceding month, along with its peer stocks, reacting to the news that the growth in the Information Technology sector was slowing down. With the negative reaction to the earnings also, the stock's P/E (price to earnings ratio too had fallen below the industry average) and the stock was trading at a 52-week low. Therefore, a bounce-back was expected for the stock from that low. Brokerage houses also gave a buy for the stock and the stock started showing signs of a reversal. A moderate 5-10% upside looked likely in the short term and therefore it was decided to go ahead with the Bull Call Spread.

Steps followed for executing the trade:

These were the steps undertaken to execute the trade.

Step 1: Select the right options to trade for the chosen stock/index.

The criteria taken into condition for determining the options to trade were:

    i. The overall risk of the position shouldn't exceed 5% of the total allocated capital (total available capital was approximately 175,000).

    ii. The lower-strike call option to be bought shouldn't be more than 5% away from the market price of the underlying stock that was at that time trading at 383. This is because the rise in stock price expected was about 5-10% in the near term and the Bull Call Spread had to stay within that range from the market price.

Taking these criteria into consideration, it was decided to trade the 400 and the 440 call options.

Step 1: Buy OTM call option

The Tech Mahindra 400 call option with June month Expiry was bought at ₹7.45.

Step 2: Sell OTM call option with higher strike-price

The Tech Mahindra 440 call option (2 strikes higher than 400 CE) with June month Expiry was sold at ₹1.6.

The table below summarises the crucial information regarding the trade:

Summary Table		
Stock or Index Traded	Tech Mahindra	
Lot size for each option	1100	
Option 1	Strike Price	400
Lower-strike Call Option - Buy	Premium Paid	₹ 7.45
Option 2	Strike Price	440
Higher-strike Call Option - Sell	Premium Received	₹ 1.60
Max Profit		₹ 37,565
Max Loss		₹ -6,435
Condition for maximum profit	Stock price at time of expiry > Strike Price of Higher-Strike Call option	
Condition for maximum loss	Stock Price at time of expiry < Strike Price of Lower-strike call option	
Break-even Price at Expiry	Stock Price at expiry = ₹ 405.85	

The tabulation shows the maximum profit that could be attained if the Tech Mahindra stock stayed above 440 at the time of expiry was ₹37,565.

Note: Max Profit = (Difference of the two strike-prices of the call options) – (Net premium paid to enter the position)] x Lot size. Thus, Max profit = [(440-400) – (7.45-1.6)] x 1100 = ₹37,565.

The total risk (maximum potential loss) was ₹6435.

Total Risk = Net premium paid for entering position x lot size = (Premium received – Premium Paid) x lot size. Therefore, this equals (7.45 – 1.6) x 1100 = ₹6,435.

The break-even point was 405.85 (lower-strike plus the net premium received, or, 400 + (7.85-1.6)). As long as the Tech Mahindra stock trades above this threshold, at the time of expiry, a profit was assured.

The profit/loss payoff diagram below shows the profit and loss plotted against five different expiry prices for the stock.

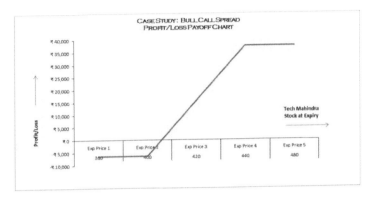

Result of the Trade:

The position was held for six days, and during this period, the underlying stock appreciated by more than 10%. The position was closed on the 6th of June when the stock was trading around the 409 mark. After the sharp rise, the position was in good profits and since only a limited upside was expected in the short term, it was a good time to exit. Final details of the trade at time of closure are shown in the table below.

Entry Date	Exit Date	No. Trading Days	Stock Price at Entry	Options Traded	Lot size	Option Strike Price	Option Buy Price	Cost Price per Lot	Option Sell Price	Sell Price per Lot	P/L per Trade Leg	Stock Price at Exit	Overall P/L
30-May	06-Jun	6	384	TechM CE	1,100	1,100	₹7.45	₹8,195	₹15.60	₹17,160	₹8,965	409	₹7,590
				TechM CE		1,080	₹2.80	₹3,080	₹1.55	₹1,705	-₹1,375		

The trade was closed for a total profit of ₹7,590

Return on Investment

The ratio of the net profit (or loss) to the sum invested in the trade will give the percentage of profit, or the ROI, from this trade.

A sum of approximately ₹60,000 was blocked by the broker as margin for selling the 440 call option in order to receive the credit of ₹1760 (premium of ₹1.6 x lot size of 1100) and a sum of ₹8,195 (premium of ₹7.45 x lot size of 1100) was paid for purchasing the lower-strike option. Therefore the total investment in this trade was ₹60,000 + ₹8,195 (sum of margin blocked + premium paid) = ₹68,195. The net profit was ₹7,590, as mentioned earlier.

Therefore, a quick tabulation shows the profit ratio as 0.11, or in other terms the trade yielded a return of approximately 11%.

PS: Broker charges were not included in the tabulation above since these were negligible.

Worksheet for the Bull Call Spread

The Bull Call Spread worksheet is the fifth worksheet in the Strategies Workbook and you can use it to paper-trade or to check profit/loss potential before you execute this strategy.

Strategy 5: The Bear Put Spread

The Bear Put Spread is a directional strategy that that can be deployed when a trader has a negative outlook on the underlying stock/index and expects it to fall moderately in the short term.

The Bear Put Spread, like the Bull Call Spread discussed earlier, is a debit spread and hence, you will need to pay a net debit to enter into the position.

How to Execute this Strategy

Step 1: Identify an optimum stock/index that fits the criteria for trading this strategy.

Step 2: Buy one slightly OTM put option.

Step 3: Sell one OTM put option that has a strike-price 1 or 2 strikes lower than the option bought in Step 1, and with the same expiry date and of the same underlying stock/index.

Monitor your position periodically and square off both options once the position has yielded significant profits (ideally, 30-40% of maximum potential profit).

Note: As it was with the Bull Call Spread, if you increase the spread, you can increase your maximum profit potential, though this would increase the risk. Likewise, when you decrease the spread, the risk decreases, but so would the maximum profit potential.

When to Use this Strategy

Trade the Bear Put Spread when the market has a negative outlook on the stock following some development such as a below-par earnings result, or in the face of an organisational change, or decision-making in the company, that is deemed negatively by investors. You can also trade this when the particular sector, the company is part of, is under selling pressure (due to some unfavourable market/environmental conditions that just surfaced).

Note: Since this is a debit spread strategy, time-decay will work against the overall position even though decay will be considerably slower than that of a naked long put position since time-decay works in favour of the lower-strike put option and thereby reduces the rate of time-decay of the overall position.

Profit and Loss Potential

The chart below shows the profit and loss payoff for a typical Bear Put Spread.

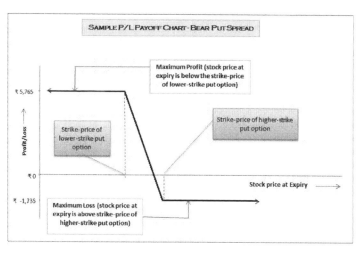

[Note: Numbers used in the chart above are indicative only.]

As shown in the chart above, maximum profit can be made on a Bear Put Spread when at the time of expiry the stock is trading below the strike-price of the lower-strike put option.

Maximum Profit = [(Difference of the two strike-prices of the put options) – (Net premium paid to enter the position)] x Lot size.

Maximum Loss is incurred on the Bear Put Spread when the price of the stock at expiry is above the strike-price of the higher-strike put option.

Maximum Loss = (Net premium paid to enter position) x Lot size.

Net Premium = Premium paid for higher-strike put option – Premium received for lower-strike put option.

Note: Brokerages, as applicable, need to be factored in to get a more accurate profit/loss calculation.

Example: A stock X was trading at 500 when a Bear Put Spread was traded using the 480 put option of Stock X and 460 put option of Stock X, both options expiring the same month. If stock X goes down and stays under 460 at the time of expiry of the options, maximum profit will be gained. On the contrary, if stock X does not fall below even 480, at the time of expiry of these options, maximum loss will be incurred.

Advantages v/s Disadvantages

In terms of advantages and disadvantages, this spread is very similar to the Bull Call Spread. The primary advantage of this trade is that it has a very good reward to risk ratio and a moderate down move by the stock can result in good profits.

You can also increase the profit potential of this spread by widening the spread (increasing the strike-prices between the two options) or you can choose to reduce the risk further by decreasing the spread (decreasing the number of strike-prices between the two options)

The disadvantage of this strategy is that time-decay works against the position and despite the limited loss potential, if the stock stays stagnant for too long, the position will end in a loss.

Case Study of a Bear Put Spread Trade

This following example shows how a Bear Put Spread was successfully traded and closed for a profit.

Entry Date: 18th of May 2017

Underlying Index: Nifty 50 (Benchmark Index of the NSE, India).

Days to Expiry left for Options (for closest monthly series): 7

Stock Exchange: National Stock Exchange (NSE), India.

Background of the traded Index: The Nifty 50 is the benchmark index of India's NSE. Trades on the Nifty have been used in other case studies in this book too.

Reasons for entering trade: The Nifty index had shown an impressive rise for over a month in-line with positive global cues (the NASDAQ had also hit all-time highs around this same time). However, the psychological 9500 mark was showing strong resistance and though the index had been hovering around the mark for many days, it didn't seem to have enough strength to breach the 9500 mark, and was trading in a narrow range. With less than a week to go for the expiry of the May month options contract, it looked highly likely that some profit booking would take place and there would be some slight correction in the near term. The option premiums were also cheap given the number of days to expiry and a Bull Put Spread could be entered with relatively low risk and looked likely to have a high chance of success.

Steps followed for executing the trade

These were the steps undertaken to execute the trade.

Step 1: Identify the right options to trade

The criteria taken into condition for determining the options to trade were:

i. The overall risk of the position was not meant to be more than 3% of the total available capital (with only 7 days left to expiry in that given month's options, option prices for options expiring that month were available at a discount – hence there was no need to risk as much as the standard 5%).

ii. Since only a moderate correction of not more than 100 points was expected in the underlying index, the slightly OTM higher-strike put option to be bought was not supposed to be more than 30-40 points below the market price of the underlying index (Nifty), which at that time was at approximately 9460.

Taking these criteria into consideration, it was decided to trade the 9450 put option and the 9300 put option that were trading at ₹40.75 and ₹13 respectively. The total risk (maximum potential loss) was only about ₹2,081 (difference of the two prices x lot size), which was only about 1.2% of the total available capital.

Step 2: Buy OTM put option

The Nifty 9450 PE with May month expiry was bought at ₹40.75.

Step 3: Sell OTM put option with lower strike-price

The Nifty 9300 PE (3 strikes lower than the 9450) with May month expiry was sold.

A summary of the trade position is shown below:

Summary Table		
Stock or Index Traded	Nifty	
Lot size for each option	75	
Option 1 Higher-strike Put Option - Buy	Strike Price	9450
	Premium Paid	₹ 40.75
Option 2 Lower-strike Put Option - Sell	Strike Price	9300
	Premium Received	₹ 13.00
Max Profit		₹ 9,168.75
Max Loss		-₹ 2,081.25
Condition for maximum profit	Stock price at time of expiry < Strike Price of lower-Strike put option	
Condition for maximum loss	Stock Price at time of expiry > Strike Price of higher-strike put option	
Break-even	Stock Price at expiry = ₹ 9,422.25	

As shown in the table above, the maximum profit that could be obtained, if the Nifty index fell below 9300 at time of expiry, was ₹9,168.75.

The maximum loss that could be incurred in the event of the Nifty index staying above 9450, at the time of expiry, was ₹2,081.25 – this is the total risk of the position, as mentioned earlier.

The break-even point price was 9422.25 (higher strike-price – the net premium received).

The profit/loss payoff diagram in the following page shows the profit and loss plotted against five different expiry prices for the index.

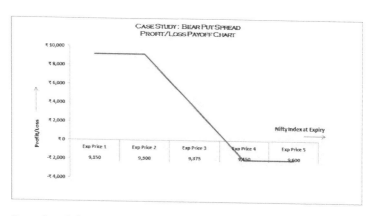

Result of the Trade

Only a day after the position was entered into, the Nifty index went down by more than 60 points, and accordingly, the price of both Nifty put options accordingly rose. Since the index was not expected to correct much further and reverse its movement before long, the position was closed by squaring of both legs of the trade and the profit was booked.

Final details of the trade at the time of closure are shown in the table below:

Entry Date	Exit Date	No. Trading Days	Index Price at Entry	Options Traded	Lot size	Option Strike Price	Option Buy Price	Cost Price per Lot	Option Sell Price	Sell Price per Lot	P/L per Trade Leg	Index Price at Entry	Overall P/L
18-May	19-May	2	9,460	Nifty PE	75	9,450	₹40.75	₹3,056	₹74.95	₹5,621	₹2,565	9,397	₹2,265
				Nifty PE		9,300	₹17.00	₹1,275	₹13.00	₹975	-₹300		

At the time of exiting the trade, the Nifty 9300 PE was trading at ₹17 and the Nifty 9450 PE was trading at ₹74.75. The overall position was considerably profitable at the time the trade was exited.

Return on Investment (ROI)

The ratio of the net profit (or net loss) to the total sum invested in the trade will give the profit percentage, or ROI, in this trade.

A sum of approximately ₹40,000 was blocked by the broker as margin for selling the 9300 put option that was sold for a total sum of ₹975 (premium of ₹13 x lot size of 75) and a total sum of ₹3,056 (premium of ₹40.25 x lot size of 75, rounded off) was paid for purchasing the 9450 put option.

Therefore, the total investment in this trade was ₹3,056 + ₹40,000 (premium paid + margin blocked for selling) = ₹43,056. The net profit was ₹2,265, as shown in the final trade summary.

Dividing the profit by the total investment shows the profit ratio to be .052, or in other terms the trade yielded a return of 5% within the duration of 2 days.

Note: Since a low-cost broker was used, the brokerages incurred were negligible and hence excluded from these calculations to keep it simple.

Worksheet for the Bear Put Spread

The Bear Put Spread worksheet is the sixth worksheet in the Strategies Workbook and you can use it to paper-trade or to check profit/loss potential before you execute this strategy.

Strategy 6: The Long Straddle/Strangle

Long straddles are an unlimited profit with limited risk options trading strategy used when a trader thinks the underlying stock/index will experience significant volatility in the near term.

Of all strategies discussed in this book, the Long Straddle is the riskiest and should be traded only in the rarest of situations when there is a huge price movement expected in a stock or index, in the near term.

That being said, this is also the strategy that has the potential to fetch you maximum profits amongst all discussed strategies in this book because there is no upper limit on the profit you can make in a Long Straddle.

Note: The Long Strangle is a slightly modified version of the Long Straddle and it is explained, in brief, later in this section.

How to Execute this Strategy

Step 1: Select a stock/index that fits the criteria for trading this strategy based on the short-term outlook for it.

Step 2: Buy an ATM call option of the chosen index/stock

Step 3: Buy an ATM put option, with the same expiry date and of the underlying stock as that of the call option purchased in Step 1.

 Monitor the trade closely and once the anticipated large price movement takes place, close both legs of the trade at the same time. Since time-decay will impact both these options, it is prudent not to hold a straddle for more than a few days.

Note: The strike-prices of both the ATM put and call options should be the same in a Straddle trade. However, when entering the trade, it may not be possible to buy the options when the market price of the stock exactly matches the chosen strike-price. In reality, the market-price of the stock may be slightly above or below the chosen strike-price of the options and therefore, one option could be slightly OTM while the other could be slightly ITM, when initiating the trade.

When to Use this Strategy

The Long Straddle/Strangle trade is meant to be used ONLY on the rarest of occasions when expecting a sharp and sudden fall/rise in the stock following the outcome of some external factor.

When entering a Long Straddle position, the trader also needs to ensure that implied volatility isn't very high (for example: greater than 60% of historical volatility), because if there is a sharp drop in volatility even after the expected stock price movement, the volatility drop will seriously hurt profit potential.

The Long Straddle can be ideally traded when there is any major policy or decision making that could have a huge impact on the underlying stock that could cause it to either rise rapidly or fall rapidly. Some of the situations in which this can be traded:

- Annual or Quarterly results of a company is due within a day or two and there are huge expectations from it.

- A major decision regarding the future of the company is due (such as decisions on an acquisition/merger or a change in top-leadership) in the next day or two.

- A major announcement regarding declaration of a large dividend or bonus issue is imminent.

If the underlying is a benchmark index (such as the Nifty), situations that can create a major rise or fall include events such as the announcement of the country's annual financial budget, major monetary policy decisions, major socio-economic decisions, and major election results.

Do not trade a Long Straddle if the underlying stock or index is trading in a narrow range, or if the outlook on the stock or index is quite neutral (or only marginally positive or negative) for the short term.

A Long Straddle should also be avoided if the implied volatility is high (say for example, the Volatility index, VIX, for that index is greater than 15) even if there is potential for a movement.

Lastly, if you have a Long Straddle position in place, exit that position as soon as that sharp rise or fall happens and you are in profits. If you hold on too long once you are in profits, you will be in danger of losing your profits because of time-decay, or because of a potential volatility drop, or both.

Profit and Loss Potential

The chart that follows shows the example of a typical profit and loss payoff for a Long Straddle trade.

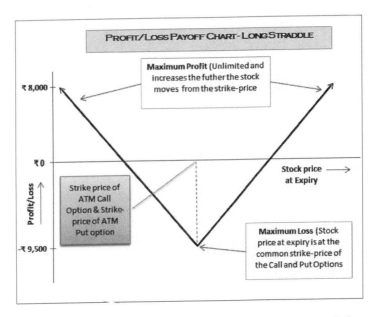

[Note: Numbers used in the chart above are indicative only.]

As shown in the chart above, when the stock makes a sharp move (rise or fall), then one side of the options will become ITM and the counterpart option will become OTM. The further (and quicker) the stock moves away from the strike (in either direction), the greater the profit. There is no ceiling for the profits that could be earned from a straddle.

Maximum Profit = Unlimited.

The loss incurred on a straddle trade is maximum when both the options expire at the strike-price and the loss is equal to the total premium paid (for both the call and put options) to enter the trade (plus brokerages, as applicable).

Maximum Loss = Total sum paid for ATM call option + Total sum paid for ATM put option.

Advantages v/s Disadvantages

The primary advantage of the Long Straddle is that it gives you a chance to earn potentially unlimited profits once the trade crosses the break-even point in either direction.

The straddle can be used to earn profits from volatile stocks without having to predict the direction in which a stock moves since it can profit from both a fall and a rise in the price of the underlying stock.

A third advantage of the straddle is that the risk exposure is limited to the total premium paid at the time of entering the trade.

The main disadvantage of the Long Straddle trade is that it faces time-decay and since this affects both legs of the straddle trade, the time-decay of the position gets compounded.

Another disadvantage is that for this position to earn a profit, there has to be a very sharp movement of the underlying stock in relatively short time (so that it outstrips the rate of time-decay) to earn profits.

The Long Strangle – a modified version of the Long Straddle

The Long Strangle is a strategy very similar to the Long Straddle in which the trader instead of buying an ATM put and an ATM call at the same strike-price, buys a slightly OTM put and a slightly OTM call for the same underlying and for the same expiry date.

The advantage of the Long Strangle, over the Long Straddle, is that the total premium that needs to be paid to enter the position will be less in the case of the Long Strangle. The trade-off is that you will need a greater move to recover your costs when compared to the Long Straddle.

You can profit from a Long Strangle when there is a sharp move by the stock similar to a Long Straddle position, and the potential profits are potentially unlimited.

Maximum loss will be incurred if the stock price settles between the call strike-price and the put strike-price at the time of expiry. The maximum loss, as in the same case of the straddle will be premium paid to buy both the call and put options.

Case Study of a Long Straddle/Strangle Trade

The following case study shows how a Long Strangle was traded and successfully closed for a profit.

Entry Date: 08th of Nov 2016

Underlying Index: Nifty 50 (Benchmark Index of the NSE, India).

Exchange: National Stock Exchange (NSE), India.

Background: The Nifty 50 is the benchmark index of India's NSE. This is an index that has been used in some of the other case studies too.

Reasons for entering trade: A very important global political change was about to take place which was highly likely to have a major short term impact on global stock markets – the US presidential elections. The US was all set to go to the polls and there was no consensus on who could be the next US president. While the media seemed to have a bias towards the Democrat candidate Hillary Clinton, there was a possibility that the Republican candidate Donald Trump could win too, against most poll predictions. A Hillary win was expected to create a huge positive sentiment in the market while a Trump win was expected to do the opposite. Either way, it looked as though the global stock markets were all poised to make a big leap forward or a giant step backward – hence, the situation looked ideal to trade the Straddle/Strangle.

Steps followed for executing the trade

These were the steps the trader undertook to execute the trade.

Step 1: Find the right options to trade.

It was decided to trade a Long Strangle on the Nifty index. Since the Nifty index was trading around the 8530 mark, the closest OTM call option was the 8550 Nifty call option and the closest OTM put option was the 8500 Nifty put option, and therefore, these two were selected for the trade –expiry dates for both were on 24th of November, which was the expiry date of the earliest expiring monthly series. While the volatility of the Nifty index was shown to be a higher-than-usual 14.9 (depicted by the India VIX volatility index), it was decided that the risk was worth taking since volatility was expected to rise even further before the big move, making the options even more expensive.

Step 2: Buy slightly OTM call option

The Nifty 8550 call option was bought for a premium of ₹130

Step 3: Buy slightly OTM put option

The Nifty 8500 put option was bought for a premium of ₹90

The table below shows the summary of the options traded as part of this trade:

Summary Table		
Stock or Index Traded	Nifty	
Lot size for each option	75	
Option 1	Strike Price	8550
Slightly-OTM Call Option : Buy	Premium Paid	₹ 130.00
Option 2	Strike Price	8500
Slightly-OTM Put Option : Buy	Premium Paid	₹ 90.00
Max Profit		No Limit
Max Loss		-₹ 16,500
Condition for maximum profit	No Upper Limit for Profits	
Condition for maximum loss	For Strangle: Stock Price at expiry lies between Strike Prices of Option 1 & Option 2	
Break-even Points	Upper	Stock price at Expiry = 8,770.00
	Lower	Stock price at Expiry = 8,280.00

While the potential maximum profit is unlimited, the maximum loss that could be incurred in this trade was ₹ **16,500** (the net premium paid for buying the two options x lot size).

There are two break-even points in the case of this trade (since profits can be earned in both directions).

The upper break-even point was **8,770** (Strike-price of call option + the net premium paid) and the lower break-even point was **8,280** (Strike-price of put option – the net premium paid).

Note: Brokerages have not been included in the calculations, since they were negligible.

The profit/loss payoff diagram below shows the profit and loss plotted against different expiry prices for the stock.

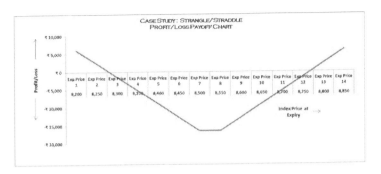

CASE STUDY: STRANGLE/STRADDLE
PROFIT/LOSS PAYOFF CHART

Note: In a Straddle trade, both the put and call options would have had the same strike-price (ATM). In this example however, since the Long Strangle was traded, there are two strike-prices involved, both slightly OTM. Accordingly, in the P/L Payoff chart, the point of Maximum Loss gets flattened out (between the two strike-prices of 8500 and 8550) instead of being a point (the common strike-price), as in the case of the Straddle.

Result of the Trade

The trade was held on for 3 days and on the 11th of November, when the US Presidential election vote count was complete and when Donald Trump won against expectations, the Indian Stock market (which was in session at the time of the result declaration) reacted negatively and the Nifty index fell by over 300 points.

The sharp fall in the Nifty index meant the Long Strangle trade went substantially into profits - while the 8550 call option premium fell from ₹130 to ₹75, the 8500 put option premium more than made up for that by rising from ₹90 to ₹295. Both positions were squared off back-to-back before the close of the trading day and the profit was booked.

Point to Note: The negative sentiment on the unexpected election results lasted for only a day and the market swung back the other way the very next day – if the trade had not been closed that same day, it would have resulted in a loss the next day due to a volatility drop and time-decay.

Final details of the trade at the time of closure are shown in the table below:

Entry Date	Exit Date	Total Trading Days	Options Traded	Lot size	Index Price at entry	Strike Price	Option Buy Price	Total Cost Price per Lot	Option Sell Price	Total Sell Price per Lot	P/L Individual Legs	Index Price at exit	Overall P/L
08-Nov	11-Nov	3	Nifty Call	75	8560	8550	₹130.00	₹9,750.00	₹75.00	₹5,625.00	-₹4,125.00	8270	₹11,250
			Nifty Put			8500	₹90.00	₹6,750.00	₹295.00	₹22,125.00	₹15,375.00		

Return on Investment

The ratio of the net profit to the sum invested in the trade will give the percentage of profit, or the ROI, in this trade.

A sum of ₹6750 (premium of ₹90 x lot size of 75) was paid for purchasing the 8500 put option and a sum of ₹9750 (premium of ₹130 x lot size of 75) was paid for purchasing the 8550 call option. Therefore, the total investment made to enter the trade was the net sum of the two amounts and was equal to ₹16,500.

The net profit of the trade was ₹11,250, as shown in the table. Therefore, a quick tabulation shows the profit ratio as 0.68, or in other terms, the trade yielded a return of 68% in three days.

Note: The brokerages incurred were negligible and hence, was not included in the tabulation above.

Worksheet for the Long Straddle/Strangle

The Long Straddle/Strangle worksheet is the seventh (and last) worksheet in the Strategies Workbook and you can use it to paper-trade or to check profit/loss potential before you execute this strategy.

The Six Strategies in a Nutshell

Now that you have gone through each of the six strategies and have also seen case studies for each of them, you should be having a fair enough understanding of each of the strategies and when to deploy them.

The table below serves as a quick-reference chart for each of these strategies. When in doubt, take a peek into this chart for guidance.

No.	Strategy Name	Type	Whether Directional	Time Decay	When to Use	Risk Involved
1	Bull Put Spread	Credit Spread	Directional	Advantage	Stock expected to rise, stagnate or fall minimally in the short term	Relatively Low
2	Bear Call Spread	Credit Spread	Directional	Advantage	Stock expected to fall, stagnate or rise minimally in the short term	Relatively Low
3	Bull Call Spread	Debit Spread	Directional	Disadvantage	Stock expected to rise moderately in the short term	Moderate
4	Bear Put Spread	Debit Spread	Directional	Disadvantage	Stock expected to fall moderately in the short term	Moderate
5	The Iron Condor	Credit Spread	Non-Directional	Advantage	Stable or range-bound stock	Low
6	Long Straddle/Strangle	Debit	Non-Directional	Disadvantage	High Probability of imminent sharp rise/fall in stock price	Relatively High

Remember that while directional debit based strategies are more likely to get you quicker and greater returns, and have a better risk to reward ratio, time-decay works against them. This is why debit spreads are less preferred among professional traders.

The Long Straddle/Strangle strategy should be used only in the rarest of situations and once the expected directional move has been triggered, the position should be squared-off as early as possible because time-decay in a Long Straddle/Strangle is accelerated given that both legs of the trade experience time-decay.

In the long run, the credit based strategies (net selling strategies) are more likely to given you smaller but more consistent returns because probability and time almost always favour them.

The Iron Condor ranks among the most favoured strategies for consistent income generation because in addition to the benefits enjoyed by the other two credit spreads such as probability and time-decay, it also has the advantage of being neutral to the direction in which the underlying stock moves.

Chapter 8: Useful Third-Party Resources

Once you get the hang of the basics of options trading, it would help you if you relentlessly kept learning to understand the intricacies of trading, and learn the numerous little techniques that could help you in executing trades better or in adjusting any trades when the need arises. Learning to trade options successfully is a skill you can use for life, and accordingly you need to keep nurturing it.

There are many internet resources that could help you understand options trading better. Here is a compact list of immensely useful resources you should look into to enhance your knowledge about options trading.

1. Udemy Courses

Udemy is among the best online paid-platforms to learn just about anything these days and there are quite a few value-for-money video courses on Udemy pertaining to options trading. These are two of the really good ones:

i. **How to win with Weekly Options**, by Jeff Tompkins, available at the URL:

http://bit.ly/UdemyCourse_JT

ii. **Options Trading Basics**, by Hari Swaminathan, available at the URL:

http://bit.ly/UdemyCourse_HS

Both the instructors provide a lot of great insight into options trading and additionally, they release videos every now and then that illustrate various little techniques in optimising various trades, among other information.

2. Top Options Trading Blogs

The following blogs host some fabulous content and are run by some of the most experienced and popular trading professionals out there:

i. **Option Pit**, by Mark Sebastian, available at the URL:

http://www.optionpit.com/

ii. **Sheridan Mentoring**, by Dan Sheridan, available at the URL:

http://www.sheridanmentoring.com/trading-blog/

iii. **Investing with Options**, by Steven Place, available at the URL:

http://investingwithoptions.com/

There are probably many other good resources on options trading out there, and if you have the inclination to explore more about options trading, by no means should you restrict yourself to just the links given above.

All being said, as a beginner, you shouldn't get overwhelmed with too much information and I would suggest you start off with just 1 or 2 resources at a time for guidance and if your time permits, to start looking at more.

3. Virtual Trading Platforms

A Virtual Trading platform is where you can get the actual feel of trading in a stock market without any risk. In these platforms, you will be allocated a generous virtual capital to do trading with. You can test various strategies here till you get the hang of trading and then venture out into actual trades on a real trading platform. Here are few popular ones you could use:

i. **How the Market works** (for virtual trading in NYSE), available at the URL:

   http://www.howthemarketworks.com/

ii. **Investopedia Stock Simulator**, available at the URL:

   http://www.investopedia.com/simulator/

iii. **NSE Paathshaala** (for virtual trading in NSE), available at the URL:

   https://www.nseindia.com/NP/nse_paathshaala.htm

A note for those trading in the US Stock market: The vast majority of the outstanding online resources (including the blogs above) are hosted by experts who trade in the US Markets. Therefore, by using these resources, you get a lot of additional insights on specific stocks and indexes in the US Markets.

Disclaimer: The resources and website links mentioned in this section are third-party resources and the author is not affiliated with any of the above in any capacity. These resources are shared with the reader for informational purposes only. Any issues/clarifications/enquiries with respect to these courses or featured podcasts will need to be taken up with the respective website owner/administrator directly.

A Final Note

If you have carefully read and understood everything that has been taught in this book, you will now be in possession of the knowledge that is required to help you confidently start trading options to earn a consistent income every month.

Undoubtedly, with your newfound knowledge you must be raring to go!

Nevertheless, do understand that while the content in this book has equipped you with valuable understanding and some excellent strategies, it is still not a substitute for hands-on experience. And this is why you should spend at least 2-3 months frequently practicing paper-trading (or trading on virtual platforms such as the ones discussed in Chapter 8) – <u>this is very important</u>.

In these first 2-3 months, observe and study the market you are trading in and focus on not more than 8-10 stocks/indexes at a time. Study their patterns of movement, check their historical levels of volatility and sensitivity to changes in the environment and paper-trade the options for these stocks. You can use the downloadable workbooks to help you with this activity too.

While carrying out your paper-trades, you are likely to make mistakes. Learn from them, so that you don't repeat those when you start doing live trading. You will also identify your areas of weakness, discover your risk appetite and learn which strategies you are comfortable with.

In general, the hands-on experience, you will gather in this period will make you a much better trader even before you risk a single dollar (or whichever currency you trade in) in the market.

Before concluding, here's a brief list of points you need to remember every time you venture out for options trading:

1. Always trade with a hedged position so that an unexpected Black Swan event doesn't end up wiping out most of your hard-earned money.

2. Take calculated risks but do not risk more than 5% of your overall capital in any single trade position.

3. Use spread-based strategies that help you calculate the potential risk and reward at the outset.

4. Define your exit points at the outset– this is important for both winning and losing trades. Keep a fixed target price at which you plan to exit your position, when in profits and also keep a price at which you plan to cut losses. Remember a primary reason why people lose money in trading is when they don't exit losing positions hoping for a turnaround. Hope isn't a strategy, so if you're losing a trade, know when to cut your losses and exit.

5. Don't expect miracles – you are much more likely to make 10 small trades that earn you $100 each than that one single trade which could earn you $1000.

6. Review all your trades after you exit – see where you went wrong (or right), learn from your mistakes.

Learning is a never-ending process and once you become a confident trader, you would most likely want to learn and experiment even more strategies.

Hope this book has met its objective in aiding you with enough knowledge, tools and confidence to venture into the world of options trading.

All the very best in your days ahead as a successful options trader!

General Disclaimer

Through this book, the author genuinely strives to teach readers the fundamentals of options trading and equip them with the necessary tools and knowledge for earning a steady alternate income. Nevertheless, this should not be interpreted as a promise or guarantee for success. Options-trading is subject to market risks and the responsibility of making the decision to invest in any trade and dealing with any positive or negative outcome solely lies with the trader. Any outcome is ultimately dependent on a variety of factors such as the trader's ability to make prudent judgements, discipline shown in trading, the outlook of the market towards the stock traded in, and the stock market environment prevalent at the time of the trade, amongst others.

Your Feedback is Valuable

Did you like this book and find it useful?

If yes, the author would really appreciate it if you could let other readers know by posting a short review. It does not matter if your review is written in a few lines or in just a few words. Your gesture will help give this book and the author the much needed exposure in a crowded market place.

You can post your review on Amazon.com by using the following URL: http://bit.ly/Review_TUOTSG

About the Author

Roji Abraham is the quintessential multi-faceted writer who loves sharing not just stories, but also his knowledge on a variety of topics with his readers. His distinctive style of breaking down and narrating ideas in a manner that could be understood by just about any reader is what makes his writing unique.

Roji Abraham has been an active participant in stock markets since 2007 and has seen his fair shares of ups and downs before investing considerable time and money to learn from the best in the business and then using his knowledge to create a healthy alternate source of income trading options while still retaining a day-job.

The author also holds a Bachelor's Degree in Electronics and Communication Engineering and an M.B.A degree from Warwick Business School, UK. He has previously published a short story collection and 2 widely respected books on the Project Management Professional (PMP®) Certification Exam.

Roji Abraham maintains an active presence on social media and you can connect with him at the following social media locales:

Twitter: http://twitter.com/RojiAbraham1
Quora: https://www.quora.com/profile/Roji-Abraham
Facebook: http://facebook.com/authorrojiabraham
Official Author Website: https://rojiabraham.com

Join the Official Newsletter

There are periodic newsletters dispatched to the subscribers of **rojiabraham.com** that provide information about the author's latest blog posts, and details of upcoming titles. These newsletter will also contain the occasional goodies like free downloads or discounts on featured titles!

You can sign up directly on the website to keep yourself informed upfront about any new announcements by the author related to Options Trading or Stock Market investments.

Made in the USA
Lexington, KY
16 August 2019